Lecture Notes in Computer Science 6473

Commenced Publication in 1973
Founding and Former Series Editors:
Gerhard Goos, Juris Hartmanis, and Jan van Leeuwen

Rob Brennan   Joel Fleck II
Sven van der Meer (Eds.)

Modelling Autonomic Communication Environments

5th IEEE International Workshop, MACE 2010
Niagara Falls, Canada, October 28, 2010
Proceedings

 Springer

Volume Editors

Rob Brennan
Trinity College Dublin
School of Computer Science and Statistics
Dublin 2, Ireland
E-mail: rob.brennan@cs.tcd.ie

Joel Fleck II
Hewlett-Packard Office of Strategy and Technology
420 Mountain Avenue, Murray Hill, NJ, USA
E-mail: joel.fleck@hp.com

Sven van der Meer
Waterford Institute of Technology (WIT)
Telecommunications Software and Systems Group (TSSG)
Cork Road, Waterford, Ireland
E-mail: vdmeer@tssg.org

Library of Congress Control Number: 2010937778

CR Subject Classification (1998): D.2, D.1, K.6, C.1.3, F.2, H.5.3

LNCS Sublibrary: SL 5 – Computer Communication Networks
and Telecommunications

ISSN   0302-9743
ISBN-10   3-642-16835-3 Springer Berlin Heidelberg New York
ISBN-13   978-3-642-16835-2 Springer Berlin Heidelberg New York

springer.com

© Springer-Verlag Berlin Heidelberg 2010
Printed in Germany

Typesetting: Camera-ready by author, data conversion by Scientific Publishing Services, Chennai, India
Printed on acid-free paper   06/3180

Preface

We are delighted to present the proceedings of the 5th International Workshop on Modeling Autonomic Communication Environments (MACE 2010). This workshop was held as part of the 6th International Conference on Network and Service Management (CNSM 2010), formerly known as and building on the success of the MANWEEK conference series. This year we met just a hundred yards away from Niagara Falls in Canada, a very exciting location.

MACE started as an experiment and over the past years has created a small yet very active community that convened again this year to discuss and evaluate new advances, innovative ideas, and solid developments. The main focus of MACE, combining modeling with communications, is certainly a hard topic that requires a lot of discussion, thus the work presented at the workshop is intrinsically debatable and might not be as practiced as in other well-established workshops, but this was the nature of MACE from the beginning. New ideas, sometimes more, sometimes less rough around the edges (and some of them even inside) are submitted and provoke extensive discussions. The field in which we are working relies on these discussions, or even adventures, and we have this year again strongly motivated and supported a variety of novel work in the technical program.

This year, the submissions, while being closely related to the main themes, brought some new areas into the workshop. We still see architectural design and the application of autonomic principles to networks and services, but we also now have submissions looking into previously unexplored areas such as Home Area Networks, multimedia streaming, virtualization, federation, and user experience. This portrays a maturity in the domain, which has by now gone through several cycles, and improves its outputs by applying the lessons learned. It seems that autonomic communications, while still being an interesting area for research, are now entering a phase of extensive exploitation. A good indicator for this is the fact that one third of the papers presented in these proceedings are based on academic-industrial collaborations rather than on purely academic research.

We are proud to present the proceedings as a volume of Springer's Lecture Notes in Computer Science (LNCS) again. This book presents the accepted papers of the technical session of MACE 2010. We had, overall, 17 submissions of which we accepted 10 as full papers. Each paper was assigned to at least four domain experts from the MACE Technical Program Committee. Furthermore, to ensure that each accepted paper provided for an interesting program and encouraged debate, we discussed all submissions and all the reviews in detail. We believe that, to support the objectives of MACE, this effort was worthwhile and we hope that this book provides you with cutting-edge ideas, thoughtfully presented solutions, as well as food for thought.

Each section of this book represents one of the technical sessions of MACE 2010. The first section, Autonomics in Home Area Networks and Multimedia, opens a new area that we have never seen before at the workshop. It includes three papers jointly written by industry (operators and equipment vendors) and academia, starting with an application of autonomic management in Home Area Networks followed by two contributions focusing on automated multimedia streaming and quality of experience for multimedia services. The second section, Ontologies, Experience, Adaptive Systems, and Federation, shows work from classic MACE areas. The four papers in this section look into ontologies and semantics for autonomic elements, address user experience, and look into architectures and governance of communication systems. The interesting twist is that, in contrast to past years, the work presented does not only address single systems but emphasizes the need to investigate federated autonomic systems. The third section, Modeling for Virtualized Infrastructure, shows the maturity of autonomic communications by demonstrating implementations of flexible network stacks, integrating context into virtual resource management, and finally applying autonomic principles for fault management in virtualized infrastructures.

We would like to thank the many people whose hard work and commitment were essential to the success of MACE 2010. Foremost are the authors who submitted their work this year. We would like to express our gratitude to the MACE Technical Program Committee and the Steering Committee for their hard work, advice, and support through all stages of the preparations for the workshop. We specifically thank all reviewers for their faith and helpful reviews. Most of the time-consuming logistical work was handled by the members of the CNSM 2010 Organization Committee, and we would like to thank the CNSM general chair, Raouf Boutaba, the Program Chairs, Hanan Lutfiyya and Yixin Diao, and last but not least, the Workshop Chair, Noura Limam, for their continuous support and help. Finally we wish to acknowledge the financial support of the CNSM sponsors, whose contributions were hugely instrumental in helping us run what we hope was a stimulating, rewarding and, most importantly, an enjoyable workshop for all its participants.

October 2010   Rob Brennan
                                                     Joel Fleck II
                                                Sven van der Meer

MACE 2010 Organization

Conference and Program Co-chairs

Rob Brennan   Trinity College Dublin, Ireland
Joel Fleck II   HP, USA
Sven van der Meer   Waterford Institute of Technology, Ireland

Steering Committee

John Strassner   POSTECH, Korea
Nazim Agoulmine   University of Evry, France
Brendan Jennings   TSSG, Ireland

Publication Chair

Tom Pfeifer   Waterford Institute of Technology, Ireland

CNSM General Chair

Raouf Boutaba   University of Waterloo, Canada

CNSM Program Chairs

Hanan Lutfiyya   University of Western Ontario, Canada
Yixin Diao   IBM T.J. Watson Research Center, USA

Publicity Chair

Carlos Westphall   UFSC, Brazil

Workshops Chair

Noura Limam   POSTECH, Korea

Finance Chair

Jin Xiao   POSTECH, Korea

Webmaster

Karthick Ramachandran   University of Western Ontario, Canada

MACE 2010 Technical Program Committee

Abdelhakim Hafid	University of Montreal, Canada
Abdelmalek Benzekri	Université Paul Sabatier, France
Ahmed Karmouch	University of Ottawa, Canada
David Lewis	Trinity College Dublin, Ireland
Declan O'Sullivan	Trinity College Dublin, Ireland
Dominic Greenwood	Whitestein Technologies, Switzerland
Dominique Dudkowski	NEC, Germany
Edmundo Madeira	UNICAMP, Brazil
Falko Dressler	University of Erlangen, Germany
Filip De Turck	Ghent University - IBBT, Belgium
Francine Krief	Bordeaux 1 University, France
Georg Carle	Technical University of Munich, Germany
James Won-Ki Hong	POSTECH, Korea
Joan Serrat	Universitat Politècnica de Catalunya, Spain
Joaquim Celestino Jnior	State University of Ceará - UECE, Brazil
José Neuman de Souza	Federal University of Ceará, Brazil
Jose-Marcos Nogueira	UFMG, Brazil
Karima Boudaoud	University of Nice Sophia Antipolis, France
Keara Barrett	Carlow IT, Ireland
Laurent Ciavaglia	Alcatel-Lucent, Bell Labs, France
Lisandro Zambenedetti Granville	UFRGS, Brazil
José Lozano	Telefónica Investigación y Desarrollo, Spain
Mark Burgess	Oslo University College, Norway
Martin Huddleston	Defence Science and Technology Lab, UK
Maurice Mulvenna	University of Ulster, UK
Mieso Denko	University of Guelph, Canada
Mikhail Smirnov	Fraunhofer FOKUS, Germany
Peter Deussen	Fraunhofer FOKUS, Germany
Roy Sterritt	University of Ulster, UK
Simon Dobson	University of St. Andrews, UK
Spyros Denazis	University of Patras, Greece
Tadashi Nakano	University of California, Irvine, USA
Yacine Ghamri-Doudane	IIE, France

Table of Contents

Design of a HAN Autonomic Control Loop

Jesse Kielthy[1], Kevin Quinn[1], Raquel Toribio[2], Pablo Arozarena[2],
Sidath Handurukande[3], Marc Garcia Mateos[4], and Martin Zach[5]

[1] Telecommunications Software and Systems Group (TSSG), Waterford, Ireland
{jkielthy,kquinn}@tssg.org
[2] Telefónica Investigación y Desarrollo, Madrid, Spain
{raquelt,pabloa}@tid.es
[3] Network Management Lab, LM Ericsson, Athlone, Ireland
sidath.handurukande@ericsson.com
[4] GMV Soluciones, Globales Internet S.A.U., Barcelona, Spain
mgmateos@gmv.com
[5] Siemens AG Austria, Vienna, Austria
martin.zach@siemens.com

Abstract. For the most part, research efforts and studies have concentrated on operators' high-capacity core networks and complex access networks. Moving beyond the access network, however, toward the outer edge and into the domain of the end-user, it is clear that a unique and equally complex set of network management problems exists.

In this paper, we present the implementation of an autonomic framework that allows operators to manage the increasingly diverse range of resources, services, protocols and standards that exist in outer edge networks.

This framework consists of critical software components that allow nodes and devices to be monitored, processed, modeled and managed within Home Area Networks (HAN). A distributed event processing component, a service modeling component, a fault management component and an innovative device adaptation layer have been integrated on a proof-of-concept testbed and are organized to capture knowledge relating to network capabilities and to provide self-managing corrective actions.

Keywords: Autonomic Network Management, Autonomic Control Loop (ACL), Future Internet, Home Area Networks (HAN).

1 Introduction

Autonomic computing is typically defined in terms of a set of "self" functions, for example: self-configuration, self-healing, self-optimization, and self-protection (i.e. self-CHOP) [1]. These building blocks can be combined to realize more powerful functions. The design of autonomic network management in an ad-hoc, heterogeneous environment such as a Home Area Network (HAN) poses many unique challenges. In addition, managing a very large number of subscribers and supporting HAN customers is a daunting and very expensive task for operators. As a result, autonomic network management in the context of HANs is a very important requirement for operators.

R. Brennan, J. Fleck II, and S. van der Meer (Eds.): MACE 2010, LNCS 6473, pp. 1–11, 2010.
© Springer-Verlag Berlin Heidelberg 2010

The role of autonomics within the HAN should be considered separate to the other functions of the HAN. For example, fault diagnosis, policy management, QoS monitoring, etc. can all take place in the HAN without any involvement of autonomics. Though the concepts presented in this paper require these functions to interact, it is important that any autonomic aspects introduced in the HAN *add value* to these existing functions.

In Section 2, an overview of autonomic architectures which have influenced the direction of the research and a select summary of some HAN-related projects is presented. This is followed in Section 3 by a high-level view of the research scenario(s) that have been designed and implemented as part of the MAGNETO project [2]. This is followed by a description of the main components of the MAGNETO autonomic framework (that are deployed within the HAN using the OSGi framework [3]]) and the MAGNETO autonomic control loop. Finally, Section 4 outlines some important conclusions, considerations and intended future work.

2 Related Work

IBM used human biology as its inspiration for autonomic computing [4]. The autonomic nervous system can monitor, check and manage the body in many ways without any conscious effort. Using this concept, IBM aimed to develop "a computing environment with the ability to manage itself and dynamically adapt to change in accordance with business policies and objectives".

The IBM control loop design includes sensors (that can monitor) and effectors (that can adjust). An Autonomic Manager (AM) provides the overall guidance for collecting, analyzing, and acting on data collected from the managed element via its sensors. The Monitor task gathers data and then presents it to the Analysis task which determines if the managed element is acting as desired. The Planning task takes this data and determines if the managed element should be reconfigured and the Execute task implements the required changes in the network [5].

The design that was conceptualized by IBM allowed networks to become more intelligent, efficient and effective. However, the focus was on IT networks and did not consider context within HANs such as the heterogeneity of devices, networks, protocols and standards, the existence of resource limited devices such as TV sets, etc.

FOCALE [6] was designed with the concept of autonomic network management in mind and therefore considers the additional constraint of heterogeneity of devices (which the IBM model did not need to consider).

The FOCALE architecture was designed to address a number of challenges, such as the inability to integrate data from different sources and the inability to dynamically adapt resources and services provided by the network.

The autonomic operation of a system or component within FOCALE is achieved using a self-learning control loop. **Fig. 1** shows a basic autonomic networking control loop. Vendor-specific data from the Managed Resource is gathered e.g. from a network node or user device, which is then analyzed to ensure that the Managed Resource is providing the appropriate services and resources at a given moment in time. If it is, monitoring continues; if it is not, then it is reconfigured and re-analyzed.

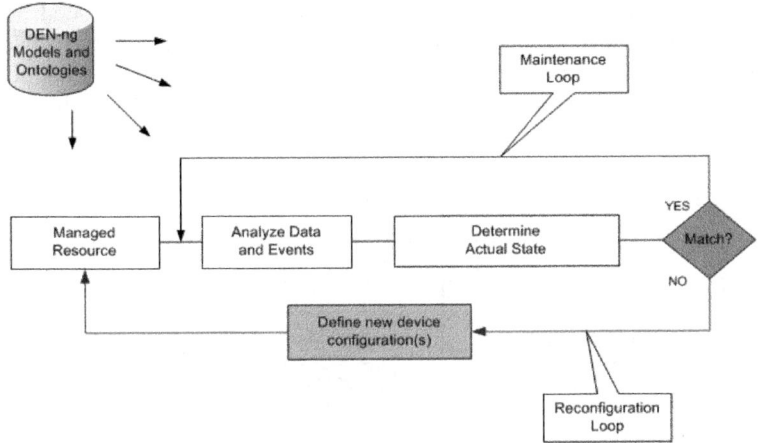

Fig. 1. Basic FOCALE Control Loop

The control loop involves comparing the current state of the Managed Resource to its desired state. If this does not match, then the Managed Resource needs to be reconfigured.

The *Generic Autonomic Network Architecture* (GANA) [7] proposes a reference model to enable standardized engineering of autonomic network devices and protocols. GANA provides a basis to realize how protocols, functions, nodes and networks can provide autonomic network management.

In Fig. 2 below, it is illustrated that at this level of self-management (autonomic) properties, the lower level *Decision-Making-Elements* (DE) operating at the level of abstracted networking functions can become the Managed Automated Tasks (*Managed-Entities* (ME)) of the main DE of the system (node).

This means the node's main DE has access to the "views" exposed by the lower level DEs and uses its overall knowledge to influence (enforce) the lower level DEs to take certain desired decisions, which may in turn further influence or enforce desired behaviors on their associated ME, down to the lowest level of individual protocol behavior.

A "Sibling" relationship simply means that the entities are created or managed by the same upper level DE. This means that the entities having a sibling relation can still form other types of peer relationship within the autonomic node or with other entities hosted by other nodes in the network, according to the protocol defined for their needs to communicate with other DEs.

The main objective of the *AutHoNe* project [8] is to design an innovative home network communication architecture with autonomous components allowing self-managing properties necessary for future home and pervasive scenarios. This new architecture will be composed of 4 planes (data, control, management and knowledge planes) allowing the system to self-configure, self-secure and self-monitor in real time so that the home-network is always optimized depending on the knowledge plane information. By distributing services throughout the home and virtually anywhere, *En-ComPAs-2* [9] aims at developing an end-to-end provisioning platform to support the communication needs of many social communities e.g., schools, local communities, hospitals, colleagues, hobbies, friends, family, etc. and for the extended home environments. *GENIO* [10] will define the home network of the future, focusing in the following main areas - *converged remote management, advanced self-management* of the home network, *ubiquitous access to home content* and subscription identification solutions *for device configuration personalization.*

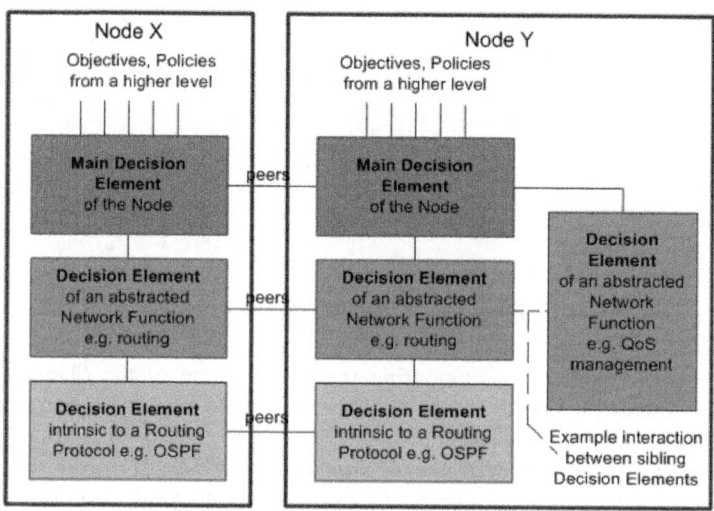

Fig. 2. Hierarchical, Peering, Sibling Relationships and Interfaces in GANA

The basic proposal of initial autonomic computing frameworks assumes that sensors can gather a comprehensive knowledge about the system. However, in HAN environments such knowledge cannot be readily obtained (within the HAN) since operators will not expose the details about edge and access networks. As a result, new approaches are necessary when devising autonomic loops for HANs; for example, it is necessary to work with "partial" knowledge about the network and to use inference techniques to handle the uncertainty that arises when "full" knowledge is not available. In addition, there are requirements in telecom networks to calculate Service Level Agreement (SLA) status. To handle such requirements there are solutions such as service modeling. As a viable solution, any autonomic loops within the HAN should be also able to combine and complement these existing requirements and solutions. The autonomic approach presented in this paper introduces methods to do this – for example, the autonomic framework co-exists and combines with service modeling components that are used to calculate the SLAs.

Other projects have focused on specific, yet equally significant, aspects within the HAN environment – EnComPAs-2 (service delivery, service continuity and profile information), GENIO (intelligence to deal with events and alarms, device configuration personalization) and AutHoNe (knowledge sharing and secure access). MAGNETO has identified other areas where research is required – namely *service centric network management* and *service assurance*. The work presented in this paper outlines the realization of a novel autonomic framework to address these two areas and provides information about some of the future development activities of the project.

3 MAGNETO

The solutions being developed in the MAGNETO project facilitate easy, reliable, secure distribution and access of content available in HANs. Ease of use, reliability and security comes as a value added service on top of normal ISP services such as connectivity, content delivery, billing, etc.

The provider of these value added services is known as the MAGNETO Service Provider (MSP) and the value added service is known as Omnipresent Virtual Network service (OVN). In short, the OVN is a virtual network built on top of existing physical networks to provide value added services to the end-users. MAGNETO addresses two main use cases: Service Degradation – which focuses on how a network can react to a degradation in the quality of a service; and Service Breakdown – which focuses on how a network can react to problems disrupting the delivery of a given service.

3.1 MAGNETO Taxonomy

Fig. 3 serves to illustrate several critical concepts regarding the taxonomy of devices in a MAGNETO context.

These are:

- *Primary MAGNETO Enabled Device* (PMED) – a MAGNETO enabled network must contain at least one PMED. Coupled with a sizeable repository (i.e. an intelligent database – see below), the PMED can centrally manage such functionality as – Fault Management, Policy Management, Autonomic Instance Manager (AIM), Security Certificate Authority (CA) and Device Discovery. The PMED also stores the autonomic software and will provide a device with access to a copy of this software when required.
- *MAGNETO Enabled Device (MED)* – a MAGNETO Enabled Device (MED) would have the necessary capabilities to install the autonomic software components from the PMED that will allow the device to participate in providing MAGNETO self-management value added services. Such intelligent devices could be laptops, desktops, data servers, high-end mobile/handheld devices, etc. Once installed, the MAGNETO components will run in an isolated and secure environment in order to have limited access to resources and to avoid the possibility of overloading and crashing the devices.
- *Non MAGNETO Enabled Device* (NMED) – a device that cannot manage itself. An association will be made to the AIM on the PMED for each of these devices.
- *Autonomic Instance Manager* (AIM) – the AIM is located on the PMED. The AIM creates a remote, logical association for each device that can not autonomically manage itself (NMEDs). The repository on the PMED will be used by the AIM to store and retrieve information about the NMED.
- *Repository* – an intelligent database that resides on each MED so they can quickly store and retrieve information. There is also a Central Repository on the PMED which allows it to store and access information that is fed back to this central point and for NMED information via the AIM. This repository will contain information relative to the configuration of the OVN, specifying which users

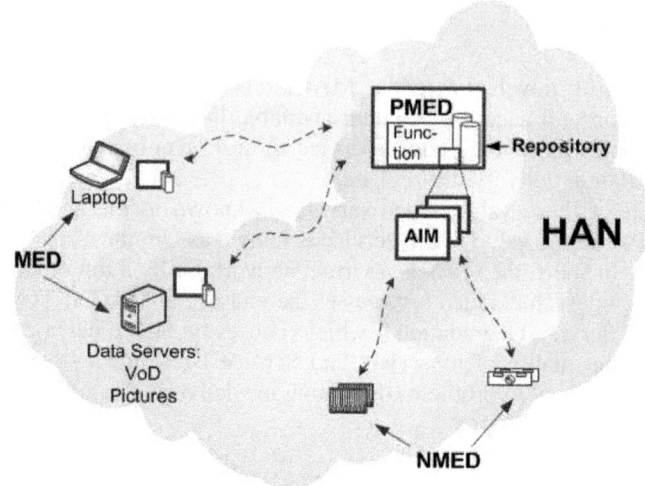

Fig. 3. PMED, MED, NMED and AIM in MAGNETO HAN

are authorized to access the OVN and which specific permissions they have to consume the shared resources; thus providing the proper privacy and integrity of such shared content.

The capabilities of new devices (e.g. capacity, processing power, etc.) that are introduced into the HAN will be discovered. At this point, it is known if the device is capable of accessing, downloading and installing the autonomic software from the PMED.

3.2 MAGNETO Autonomic Framework

To realize the autonomic vision within MAGNETO, the framework is designed with interconnected components that manage the HAN devices to deliver the best performance results for the service.

As shown in Fig. 4, MAGNETO considers a simple "Control Logic" component for the purposes of implementing corrective actions. A bi-directional Device Adaptation Layer (DAL) is presented that communicates with other MAGNETO modules mainly through exchanging events.

Low level events are sent to the Distributed Event Processing Component via the DAL which facilitates correlation within and across HANs. Resulting output events are propagated to the Modeling Component and Fault Management Component. The Fault Management Component uses these events to identify faults using Bayesian approaches [11] while the Modeling Components uses these events to provide a real-time model of the end-to-end service and provide a real-time evaluation of Service Level Agreements (SLA).

Once the Fault Management component has diagnosed a symptom, it will send the result back to the Event Processing component so an autonomic action can be applied to the network device to optimize the service or repair the fault.

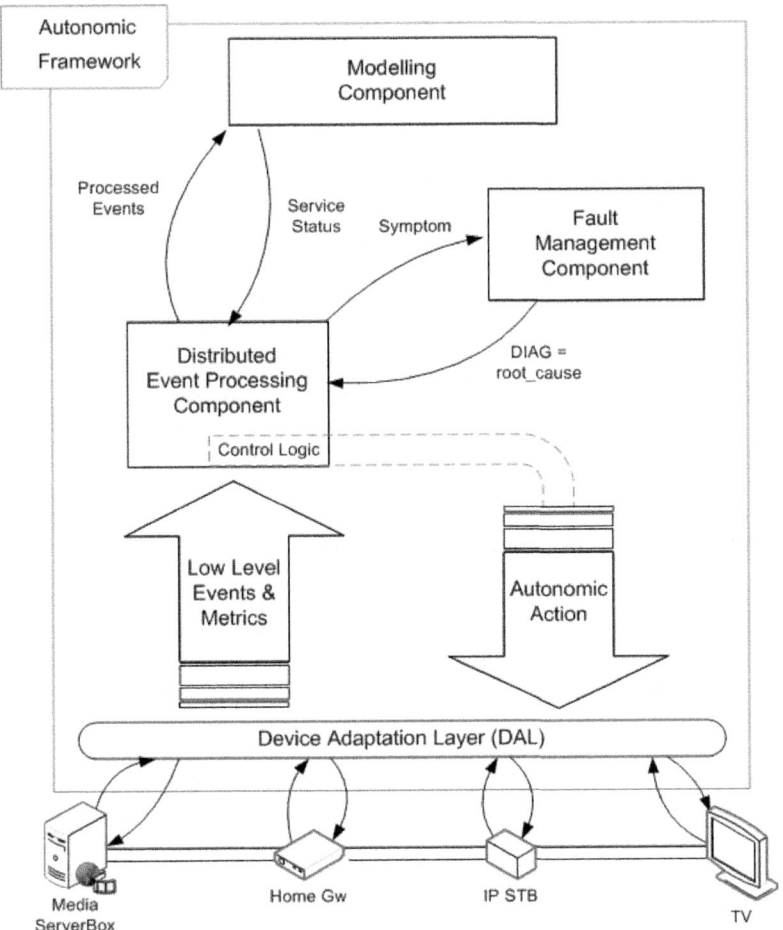

Fig. 4. Realizing a MAGNETO Autonomic Loop

In a MAGNETO Autonomic Control Loop (ACL) the system is designed to monitor and sense changes in the HAN via the active probing of low level network events and key performance metrics. The ACL also allows the system to analyze the data and model the service(s), detect any QoS infringements or errors on the network and enables the system to optimize or repair the service by taking corrective actions.

In the following sections the main MAGNETO components are described.

Device Adaptation Layer (DAL)

This component implements the device specific mediation between existing interfaces on devices and other MAGNETO components. The following events are supported in the DAL:

- Forwarding low level events from the devices
- Receiving events to be displayed at the device
- Receiving events that are to be transformed into commands to devices
- Forwarding responses to commands from the devices

A critical part of the DAL is the *capabilities interrogation* interface. This interface identifies the version of the adaptation layer definition, implements the mandatory interrogation functionality and allows for optional interrogation functionality. Knowing the version, we know what can be requested from the device and the options that may be present. With this interface in place, any other (allowed) device may get an accurate idea of what the device supports: type of device, capabilities, interaction standards, user interfaces. The rest of the capabilities and features of the device are regarding consuming the media and are just used by the network.

In the MAGNETO project we have developed a DAL for an IP-enabled STB and VLC client [12] to fetch and to push relevant information and commands to and from the network devices.

Distributed Event Processing (EP) Component

Other MAGNETO components can send a defined set of input events to the event processing component, dynamically add, delete and modify specific event processing statements, and subscribe for output events from event processing that contain higher level and semantically richer information for further use on the service management layer.

The capability to dynamically manage the event processing statements together with the power of expression of the Esper Event Processing Language (EPL) [13] also facilitates a context sensitive and adaptive way of processing events, arising from low level sources like devices and network elements as well as higher logical layers.

To allow propagation of events and distributed (stepwise) event processing, the concept is also extended for targeting subscribers at remote hosts (though these hosts do exist within the MAGNETO OVN). This event propagation can be logically considered as part of event processing, because it can be – at least partly – defined by corresponding event processing statements. The main idea of for event propagation in MAGNETO is to route events based on topics within the MAGNETO network; in this way each event processing agent only receives event types which are of interest.

The Event Processing component is based on the open-source Complex Event Processing (CEP) component *Esper*. Similar to other MAGNETO components, the Event Processing component is realised as an OSGI bundle, utilising the communication infrastructure and event handling provided by OSGI. For communication between MAGNETO nodes, as required for distributed event processing, the JADE agent framework [14] is used that supports the exchange of Agent Communication Language (ACL) messages.

Modeling Component

The Service Modeling Component represents the relationships between Key Performance Indicators (KPIs), Service Levels, Service Level Agreements (SLAs) and their associations to various network devices or to end users (when relevant). Based on these associations, the component collects and processes performance data captured at network devices.

The Modeling component is realized by the SALMon [15] engine and is a time-based computational process. The input to the process is a service model defined by the SALMon language that describes inputs, attributes and properties, relationships between components and computational statements. The model is defined using the SALmon language and is executed on top of SALmon modeling engine. It evaluates the SLAs status over time and reports to the MSP [16].

The interface is based on SOAP web services. The server exposes a Web Services Description Language (WSDL) [17] for client code generation. This is bundled as an OSGI bundle by the event processing component in order for it to send events to the modeling component.

This bundle subscribes to the *Event Admin* service for one specific event topic ("Service Model Input") that represents inputs to the SALMon Service Modelling / Monitoring Component. After receiving an event of this type it converts the event attributes to the actual inputs required by SALMon and invokes the corresponding methods of the Web Service. Sensor components have been developed to feed the modeling engine, which is a part of the autonomic framework, with events related to higher level service quality issues (e.g., video impairments) and low level network problems (e.g., packet loss, jitter).

Fault Management Component

The fault diagnosis functionality within MAGNETO is conceived as a distributed functionality that is accomplished by means of specialized agents distributed among different network elements that will collaborate in order to come up with a common goal: the diagnosis of network and service problems. The diagnosis procedure is based on probabilistic techniques, proved to be adequate to deal with uncertainty. In specific, it is based on Bayesian inference.

There are different types of agents (which are described in [18]) – the *OSGI interface* agents which serve as interface with other components; *Diagnosis* agents which receive diagnosis requests, together with observations made for the diagnosis; *Observation* agents which provide observations by performing specific tests upon request; *Belief* agents which provide a belief on a certain node state; and *Knowledge* agents which are in charge of distributing diagnosis knowledge to all interested agents and performing Self Learning by processing the results of past diagnoses.

In order to implement the multi-agent diagnosis system introduced in the previous sections, the WADE/JADE multi-agent architecture is used. This agent platform can be distributed across machines which do not even need to share the same OS. JADE is FIPA (Foundation for Intelligent Physical Agents) compliant [19] and it is completely implemented in Java language. WADE environment runs on top of JADE and provides an important mechanism to manage the deployment of the system agents. In MAGNETO, WADE/JADE agents are deployed as an OSGI bundle.

4 Conclusions and Future Work

The primary goal of MAGNETO is to design and develop an innovative distributed management framework and service management approach that will enable integrated service and network management for outer edge devices in emerging networks.

The work presented in this paper is a work-in-progress so, for this initial phase, we have concentrated solely on the management and representation of information within a single domain that has allowed for proof-of-concept development. As described in the above section, we have built the components and the prototype framework that aptly demonstrates the feasibility and practicality of our solution. We consider a scenario where one HAN user streams IPTV content to another HAN (user) through an emulated ISP network. IPTV content is streamed from a multi-media server in the source HAN (i.e. from the *Media ServerBox*) which is capable of streaming using Real Time Streaming Protocol / Real-time Transport Protocol (RTSP/RTP). In the destination HAN, an Internet Protocol (IP) enabled STB captures the stream. HANs are connected to the emulated ISP using emulated Home Gateways (HGw). Monitoring of the IPTV service quality is carried out in the MSP. The data for this is received from distributed collectors on the STB, HGw and at end-user devices (e.g., laptop).

Two further fault scenarios are currently being investigated as part of the second phase of development and they focus on a potential CPU failure on the media server box and also connectivity loss between the server box and end-user device(s). They also aim to enhance the end-user experience through the feedback of information and possible interactive features.

With further scenarios planned, MAGNETO is confident that a fully distributed solution can be delivered before the end of the project.

Acknowledgments. This paper describes work undertaken in the context of the CELTIC MAGNETO project, which is partially funded by the Spanish "Ministerio de Industria, Turismo y Comercio" under the Avanza program, by "Enterprise Ireland" as part of the International Collaboration Support Programme and by the Austrian FFG (Basisprogramme, Projekt Nr. 820360).

References

1. Kephart, J.O., Chess, D.M.: The Vision of Autonomic Computing. Computer 36(1), 41–50 (2003)
2. Management of the outer edge,
   http://projects.celtic-initiative.org/-magneto/
3. OSGi The Dynamic Module System for Java,
   http://www.osgi.org/Main/HomePage
4. An architectural blueprint for autonomic computing (June 2006),
   http://www-01.ibm.com/software/tivoli/autonomic/
   pdfs/AC_Blueprint_White_Paper_4th.pdf
5. van der Meer., S., et al.: Emerging principles of autonomic network management. In: Modelling Autonomic Communications Environments, ser. 2, Dublin, Ireland, October 2006, vol. 1, pp. 29–48 (2006)

6. Strassner, J., Agoulmine, N., Lehtihet, E.: Focale: A novel autonomic networking architecture. In: Latin American Autonomic Computing Symposium (LAACS), CampoGrande, MS, Brazil (2006)
7. Chaparadza, R., et al.: Creating a viable Evolution Path towards Self-Managing Future Internet via a Standardizable Reference Model for Autonomic Network Engineering. In: Towards the Future Internet - A European Research Perspective, pp. 136–147. IOS Press, Amsterdam (2009) ISBN 978-1-60750-007-0
8. Autonomic Home Networking (AutHoNe), http://www.authone.de/cms/
9. Enabling Community Communications–Platforms and Applications phase 2 (EnComPAs-2), http://projects.celtic-initiative.org/encompas_2/
10. Next Generation Home (Genio), http://www.celtic-initiative.org/Projects/GENIO/default.asp
11. Barco Moreno, R.: Bayesian modelling of fault diagnosis in mobile communication networks. Universidad de Málaga, Tech. Rep. (2007)
12. VideoLAN Client, http://www.videolan.org/vlc/
13. Event Stream Intelligence, http://esper.codehaus.org/
14. Java Agent Development framework (JADE), http://jade.tilab.com/
15. Wallin, S., Leijon, V., Ehnmark, J.: SALmon - A Service Modeling Language and Monitoring Engine2. In: Proceedings of the Fourth IEEE International Symposium on Service-Oriented System Engineering (SOSE), pp. 202–207. IEEE Computer Society, Los Alamitos (December 2008)
16. Handurukande, S., Wallin, S., Jonsson, A.: IPTV Service Modelling in Magneto Networks. In: 5th IFIP/IEEE International Workshop on Broadband Convergence Networks (BcN 2010), Osaka, Japan (April 19, 2010)
17. Web Services Description Language (WSDL), http://www.w3.org/TR/wsdl
18. Arozarena, P., et al.: Probabilistic Fault Diagnosis in the MAGNETO Autonomic Control Loop. In: Autonomous Infrastructure, Management and Security (AIMS 2010). University of Zurich, Switzerland (June 21-25, 2010)
19. Foundation for Intelligent Physical Agents (FIPA), http://www.fipa.org/

Towards Automated Analysis and Optimization of Multimedia Streaming Services Using Clustering and Semantic Techniques

Liam Fallon[1], Yangcheng Huang[1], and Declan O'Sullivan[2]

[1] Network Management Lab, LM Ericsson, Athlone, Co. Westmeath, Ireland
{Yangcheng.Huang,Liam.Fallon}@ericsson.com
[2] Knowledge & Data Engineering Group (KDEG) - Trinity College Dublin, Ireland
Declan.OSullivan@cs.tcd.ie

Abstract. This paper presents an automated approach for analysis and optimization of multimedia streaming services in telecommunication networks that can be used to autonomically manage those services. In the approach, threshold analysis is applied to reported quality metric values for services. Cluster analysis is then applied to the metrics to group metric values with similar characteristics. The resulting clusters are then semantically mapped to various ontologies to highlight service aspects which can be optimized with policies. Changes in service aspects are monitored to assess the effectiveness of applied optimizations.

Keywords: Multimedia; Streaming; Semantic; Service; Quality.

1 Introduction

Many of the telecommunication services available today such as IPTV, VoIP, and Video Conferencing are delivered using multimedia streams. Such services are complex and are carried over a set of highly heterogeneous networks to fixed and mobile devices and users. In the case of mobile networks, throughput can vary due to radio interference and changes of the load in cells. Wireless access technologies such as GPRS or HSDPA have different maximum limits on bit rate; inter-system handover of sessions may result in significantly different link characteristics. The dynamic nature of such factors can cause fluctuations in the quality of multimedia streams.

The orthodox approach to service analysis and optimization, such as is described for *Service Quality Monitoring & Impact Analysis (SQMIA)* applications in the TM-Forum's[1] *Telecom Applications Map (TAM)*[1] is to periodically collect information in the form of events and counters from networks and service end points, carry out an analysis on that information, and use that analysis to make improvements to the network and service end points. Although some steps

---

[1] http://www.tmforum.org

R. Brennan, J. Fleck II, and S. van der Meer (Eds.): MACE 2010, LNCS 6473, pp. 12–23, 2010.
© Springer-Verlag Berlin Heidelberg 2010

in this process such as information collection are automated, the entire process and many steps in it lack automation, requiring manual intervention by network and service experts.

This paper presents a new two-phase process for iteratively analyzing and optimizing multimedia streaming services. The first phase implements the *Analyse* part of a MAPE loop[2], with the second phase implementing the *Plan* part. The process uses *service aspects* to represent the many points of view from which sub-optimal service quality may be examined. Sub-optimal service quality may be clustered in certain regions of a network topology, so it may be useful to examine a network topology aspect. Alternatively, a geographical aspect might show that some sub-optimal service quality clusters are close together. An examination of a network inventory and software aspect might show clustering on network elements of a certain type running a particular version of software. It may even be interesting to examine sub-optimal service quality from the aspect of maintenance team zones of responsibility to see if some teams perform better than others. Each aspect is modelled as an ontology, so an ontology is instantiated for each aspect.

The *Service Quality Feedback Analysis* phase of the process analyses quality metrics from networks using a combination of threshold analysis, clustering analysis, semantic annotation and semantic mapping. Threshold analysis reduces the amount of data to be analysed by dropping metrics that reflect good quality. The novel clustering algorithm groups suboptimal metrics with similar characteristics together, thus preparing a structured dataset. Each clustered metric is semantically annotated with a reference to an ontology representing a service aspect, an approach previously used for analysing sensor data[3] but novel in its application to network metrics. Each service aspect is examined by mapping the semantically annotated clusters to the respective ontology for each service aspect using the method described in [4].

The *Service Session Shaping* phase of the process uses the mapped service aspects to apply optimizations to multimedia streams by modifying policies to be applied to the networks. The change in service aspects over successive iterations of the process is used to evaluate if policy optimizations applied to streams should be confirmed or rolled back.

We believe the process is practical because the early steps of the analysis phase are highly efficient in reducing the dataset size and clustering the data for the later less efficient semantic steps. The process is envisaged for multimedia streaming services but it is applicable to analysis and optimization of any telecommunication service. The process is also inherently autonomic in that it is iterative, the first phase reflects the *Analysis* function and the second phase reflects the *Plan* function of the MAPE loop.

The rest of this paper is organized as follows. Section 2 gives an overview of service quality management, describes some challenges with managing the quality of multimedia streams, surveys some related work, and outlines some technologies for use in service quality management. Section 3 describes our approach for automated analysis and optimization of service quality. Section 4 gives our conclusions and describes further work to be undertaken.

2   Background and Related Work

In this section, we describe the field of Service Quality Management, explaining the particular problems in managing the quality of multimedia streaming services and describing some related work. We go on to outline some technologies that can be applied to the field.

2.1   Service Quality Management

The TM Forum's *Telecom Applications Map (TAM)*[1] describes the functions that *Service Quality Monitoring & Impact Analysis (SQMIA)* applications should have as *Service Quality Monitoring, Service Quality Analysis,* and *Service Constraint Identification, Reporting, and Improvement.* Service knowledge is central to the operation of these functions, consisting of a *service model* following a standard such as the TM Forum SID[5] and service instance data in a database. Fig. 1 shows how a SQMIA compliant system assesses and improves service quality. The TAM specifies two related applications. *Service Performance Management* is responsible for collecting, collating, and archiving the information that SQMIA uses from the network and from service end points. *Service Level Agreement Management* manages the service agreements between a service provider and their customers and sets the goals for services in SQMIA.

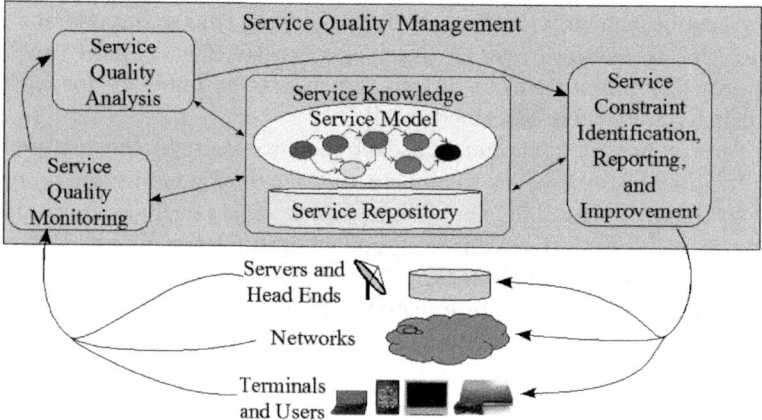

Fig. 1. Service Quality Management in the TM-Forum Telecom Applications Map[1]

The specification of the SQMIA applications in the TAM is high level. The applications are exercised in the *Service Quality Management* process of eTOM[6]. The *Service Overview Business Entity Definitions* of the SID is an extensive data model that can be used in SQMIA applications.

Service Quality Monitoring. Service Quality information may emanate from servers and head ends providing services, from networks carrying services, and from terminals and even service users. This information is collected by domain managers and is extracted by the SQMIA Service Quality Monitoring function.

Monitoring of events and statistics from network nodes is an important and accessible source of data for assessing the quality being delivered by resources carrying services. Metrics such as packet loss, delay, and jitter are available as well as information on network events such as equipment failures and overloads. Network nodes may also provide information on logical entities such as VLANs and MPLS tunnels that are carrying streams.

Information collected from service head end equipment and servers provides further insight on service quality. Such systems represent the end point of user to network services and report metrics on one end of service sessions. Information on service quality, service behaviour, and user session behaviour is often available.

Service metrics from terminals give measurements of the actual service quality being experienced by the user of a service. Quantitative metrics such as packet loss, delay, and jitter may be available. Some terminals use algorithms to estimate the perceived quality of the streaming sessions[7]. Qualitative reports on service quality solicited from users using techniques such as on-screen feedback forms may be available.

Service Quality Analysis. The quality expectation of a telecommunication service at it's point of delivery is usually well known and is typically standardized; for the voice telecommunication service the ITU-T simply specifies a set of five categories ranging from *Best* to *Poor*[8], for the IPTV telecommunication service the ITU-T specifies a large set of requirements that cover functions such as channel switch, pause and rewind as well as video and audio[9].

A wide variety and quantity of service quality related metrics are collected from network equipment. Network metrics relate to resources carrying data flows rather than multimedia streams themselves because streams flow end to end across network resources. Using network quality metrics to assess the quality of streams carrying services is a challenging task[10].

One approach is to use a set of standard network parameters as input into a mathematical model that calculates a metric indicating the quality of the service. The ITU-T uses this approach to assess voice quality: the *E-model*[11] uses a set of transmission parameters to calculate the *R-factor*, a metric ranging from 0 to 100 which gives a linear assessment of speech quality. This approach works well for voice carried over circuit switched networks because voice is a telecommunication service with a single facet (audio) and circuit switched networks are rather homogeneous in their structure. It is harder to apply this approach to services such as IPTV which have many facets (audio, video, control etc.) because sub-metrics for the quality of each facet must be determined and then those sub-metrics must be used to calculate an overall metric for the service. The ubiquity of heterogeneous packet switched networks poses another problem for this approach because it is more difficult to build mathematical models for such networks. The *E-model* specification [11] describes some limitations of its model in cases of high packet loss and high burstiness.

The use of *key performance indicators (KPI)* and *key quality indicators (KQI)* as defined in the TM Forum SLA handbook [12] are well established for assessing service quality. The metrics from networks or servers that are important for assessing service quality are identified as KPIs. KQIs are aggregates of KPIs, "usually expressed as a percentage of customers, resources or telecom entities (like a call or a session) meeting a certain level of quality"[12]. KPIs and KQIs are widely researched[13][10] and deployed in management products[14][15][16]. They work well when a service is using physical or logical network resources exclusively because it is possible to map KPIs from those resources to service KQIs. In today's networks where resources are shared by many services, KPIs and KQIs are more difficult to apply because there is no fixed mapping from resources to services. This is a particular problem in the case of counter-based statistics. If a network element merely reports the amount of packets being dropped as a KPI on an interface, it is very difficult to deduce corresponding KQIs for the various mulitmedia streams using that interface.

It is possible to use techniques such as weighting, grouping, and statistics to estimate the service quality of multimedia streaming services in the network or regions of the network[17][18]. The drawback is that the weights, groups, and statistical techniques must be tuned for the particular services and network infrastructure of each individual operator. Because such knowledge is embedded in the management system, it is not readily available for automated optimization. An enhancement of this approach is to correlate network metric values with information from multimedia streaming servers and network topology to reconstruct streams and calculate service quality on the reconstructed streams[19], allowing services and service sessions to be analysed. However, it too must be tuned for a given operators' services and networks. The correlation process described in [19] is time consuming so near real time feedback is not realisable.

Service Constraint Identification, Reporting, and Improvement. The TAM[1] defines the SQMIA role of *Service Improvement* functions as using the results of Service Quality Analysis to recommend service improvements and the role of *Service Constraint Identification and Reporting* functions as identifying and reporting areas of service deterioration to the resource layer. SQMIA systems[14][15][16] recommend service improvements and identify service constraints in networks and send reports to service planning and network planning systems.

2.2   Technologies for Service Quality Management

Threshold Analysis: A useful approach as a first pass mechanism to reduce the volume of information to be analysed. Common thresholds are set for each metric and if a metric meets that value, it is deemed to be satisfactory for all services. For example threshold analysis might be configured so that all packet loss ratio metrics below 2% are ignored. This simple mechanism eliminates all but abnormal metric values from consideration.

Clustering Analysis: A common technique for statistical data analysis[20][21]. It is used to assign a set of values into subsets so that values in each cluster are similar in some sense. It has been widely used in many fields, including machine learning, data mining, pattern recognition, image analysis and bio-informatics. We have not found any literature describing an application of these techniques to service quality management in telecommunications.

Semantic Approaches: Ontologies can be used to understand and reason about a knowledge domain. There are many ontologies in existence[2] that might be useful in understanding aspects of the service quality information data set. Semantic annotation as applied by Sheth et al.[3] is an interesting way of adding semantic references to information. Semantically tagged information can then be mapped to ontologies using the approach described in [4].

3   Automated Analysis and Optimization

We propose a process for automatically analyzing and optimizing multimedia streaming service quality that works in near real time. The process maps to the Analyse and Plan parts of an autonomic MAPE loop. The process is implemented as two phases that run periodically[3]. The *service quality feedback analysis* phase analyses sub-optimal service quality metric values collected since the last iteration of the process and semantically maps them to service aspects. The *session shaping* phase uses the service aspect maps from the analysis phase to adjust the deployment of multimedia service sessions dynamically and to monitor those adjustments to ensure they are beneficial. Adjustments that are not beneficial are rolled back. The analysis phase is implemented in the Service Quality Analysis function of TAM SQMIA, and the adaptation phase is implemented in the Service Service Constraint Identification, Reporting, and Improvement function.

Table 1 is an initial non-exhaustive list of typical service aspects.

3.1   Phase 1: Service Quality Feedback Analysis

The Service Knowledge of the SQMIA function (Fig. 1) contains service quality metric values that have been gathered from users, terminals, network equipment, servers, and head ends by the SQM Service Quality Monitoring sub-function. Service Quality Feedback Analysis uses the steps shown in Fig. 2 to identify problems with multimedia streaming services.

---

[2] See, for example, http://protegewiki.stanford.edu/wiki/Protege_Ontology_Library
[3] We assume 5 minute periods, a frequently used network statistic collection interval

Table 1. Initial List of Typical Service Aspects

Service Aspect	Description
Topology	Network topology and inventory
Geography	Physical location
Responsibility	Persons or teams responsible for entities
Demographic	Characteristics of people in an area (from census data)
Meteorology	Weather and atmospheric characteristics
Events	Concerts, sporting events, or other large gatherings
Financial	Income/Expenditure of people in an area

Fig. 2. Steps in the Analysis Phase

Initial Filtering and Threshold Analysis. In step $i)$ service quality metric values of interest are read from the service repository. Threshold analysis is used in step $ii)$ to check the values of each metric against its service quality goals. Values identified as meeting threshold goals are used to calculate the values of the clustering s and d parameters used in step $iii)$ and are dropped from further analysis.

Clustering Analysis. Suboptimal values identified by step $ii)$ are clustered in step $iii)$ using the algorithm in Fig. 3. The maximum variance d is the range inside which values must fall in order to be considered a cluster. The minimum cluster size s is the least number of values that must be in range d in order to constitute a cluster. Values falling outside a cluster are deemed to be outliers and are ignored.

The algorithm traverses the range of values for each metric from the lowest to the highest value. At $a)$ only $p1$ is in range so no cluster exists as less than s values are in range. At $b)$, $p2$, $p3$, and $p4$ are in range, a cluster is formed because s values are in range. At $c)$, $p3$, $p4$, and $p5$ are in range and because $p3$ and $p4$ are already in a cluster, $p5$ is added to that cluster. At $d)$, $p5$ and $p6$ are in range but because less than s values are in range, the cluster is not extended. Finally, at $e)$, $p6$ and $p7$ are in range; a new cluster is not formed because less than s values are in range.

Semantic Annotation and Mapping to Service Aspects. In step $iv)$ of Fig. 2, every sub-optimal cluster value is semantically tagged with a reference to the ontology representing each service aspect relevant for that value. If clusters are being examined from network topology and geographical aspects, each value

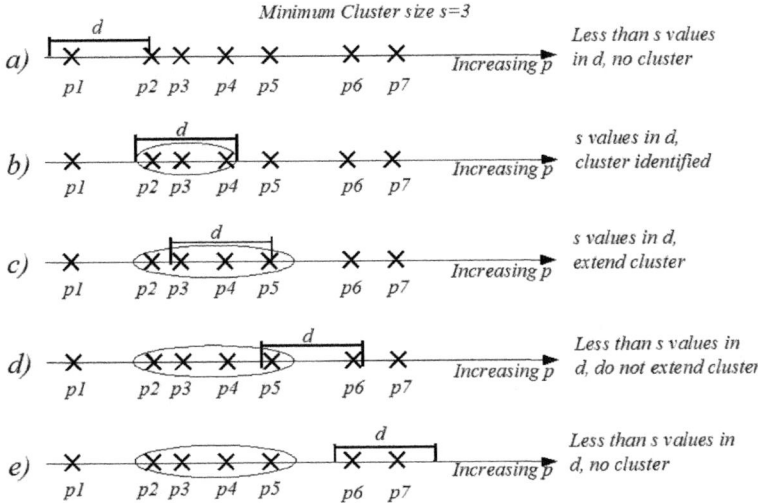

Fig. 3. The Clustering Algorithm

is annotated with a reference to an individual in the network topology ontology and with a reference to a location in the geographical ontology respectively.

The feedback clusters are mapped to each ontology representing a service aspect in step *v)*. This allows the clusters to be examined from the aspect represented by the ontology. This step is shown in more detail in Fig. 4, which shows semantic mapping for five clusters *cp1*, *cq1*, *cq2*, *cr1*, and *cr2* for three metrics *p*, *q*, and *r* to two aspects, *network topology* and *location*.

Examining the network topology aspect mapping shows that clusters *cp1* (x symbols) and *cr1* (black hexagons) are indeed located in a certain region of the network topology, indicating that there may be a network condition such as congestion in those regions. The network topology aspect also reveals that cluster *cq2* (white triangles) maps to a particular type of network element, indicating a possible configuration problem with nodes of that type. However, it is not possible to draw any conclusions on clusters *cq1* (black triangles) or *cr2* (white hexagons) from the network topology aspect.

An examination of the location aspect reveals that cluster *cq1* is geographically located on equipment in large cities, perhaps indicating a load problem with those nodes. Cluster *cr2* is highly localised, possibly indicating a problem with environmental conditions such as heavy rainfall in that location. It can also be observed that clusters *cp1* and *cr1* are localised, but that the location aspect is not particularly relevant for cluster *cq2*.

In the final step, step *vi)* from Fig. 2, the change in each aspect since the last iteration of the process is determined using inference between the ontological maps from those two iterations. The difference map is used by session shaping to apply and monitor optimizations to service delivery.

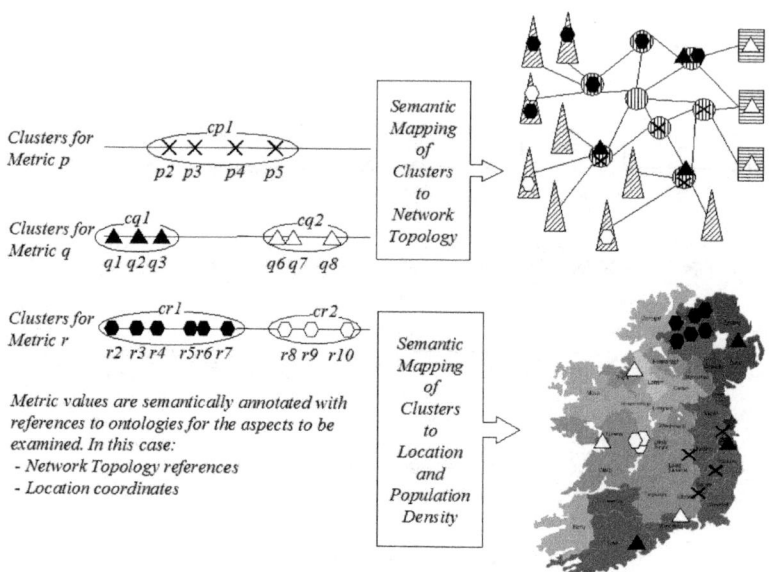

Fig. 4. Semantic Mapping of Clusters

3.2   Phase 2: Service Session Shaping

Session shaping uses the results of *service quality feedback analysis* for the current and previous iterations to decide whether and how to adapt multimedia streams.

There are many actions that can be applied to networks, terminals, and service servers to shape multimedia sessions. Traffic routing, session admission control, QoS tuning, and bit rate adaptation are examples of such actions. The appropriate action depends on the type of metric being considered, the service to which that metric applies, and the aspect of the service being considered. Session shaping may use one or a number of available adaptation actions for metrics on each cluster. These methods may be called in sequence until service quality is improved. We assume a policy based management system (PBMS) is in place for executing changes on the network. Session shaping generates policy optimizations on the policy set of the PBMS, thus propagating changes to the network.

Fig. 5 illustrates session shaping. It shows the network topology and location aspects produced by service quality feedback analysis for three iterations of the process as well as the inferred difference maps for each aspect from iteration to iteration.

On examining the aspect maps from iteration *n*, session shaping applies policy optimizations to clusters *cp1* (x symbols), *cq1* (black triangles), *cq2* (white triangles), and *cr1* (black hexagons). Session shaping does not apply an optimization to *cr2* (white hexagons) because it is deduced that the cause was probably an environmental factor such as heavy rain.

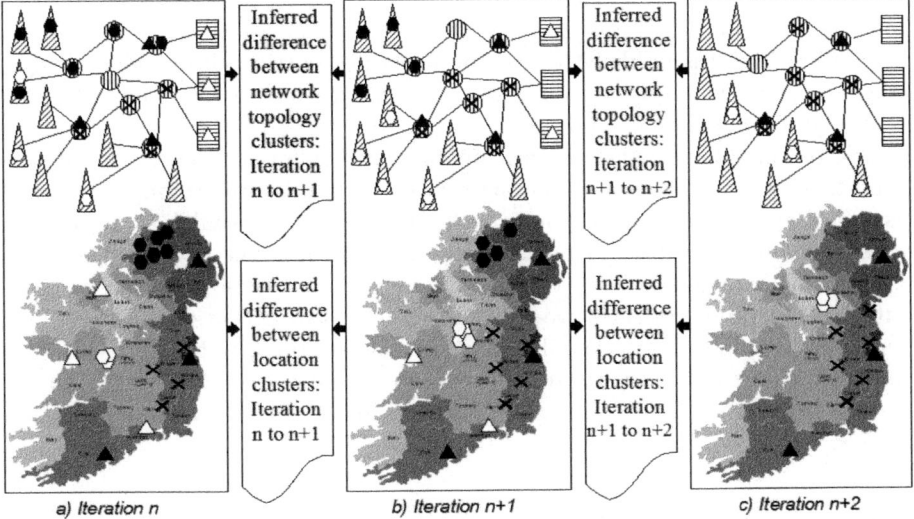

Fig. 5. Session Shaping

As it examines the inferred difference maps for iteration $n+1$ and $n+2$, session shaping observes that the optimizations for $cq2$ (white triangles) and $cr1$ (black hexagons) have been effective, the clusters reduce in size or disappear so the policy optimization is confirmed. However the policy optimizations applied to clusters $cp1$ (x symbols) and $cq1$ (black triangles) have either been ineffective or have caused service quality to deteriorate so those policy optimizations are rolled back.

The decision not to apply an optimization to $cr2$ (white hexagons) has been justified because a localised effect is seen moving north eastwards across the location aspect map, indicating the passage of the heavy rain.

4   Conclusions and Further Work

In our work to date we have seen that the Monitor and Execute steps of the autonomic MAPE loop are highly automated in network management systems today, the Analyse and Plan steps are not. The two-phase process presented here can be applied to analyse and optimize multimedia streaming services in an autonomic loop in near real time, thus closing the MAPE loop. The first phase produces views of various aspects of a service. The second phase uses the changes in those service aspects to optimize service quality over time.

The work presented in this paper is ongoing research and there are a number of topics being actively pursued.

Our analysis approach, shown on Fig. 2, uses threshold analysis and clustering analysis to reduce the amount of metrics that feed through to latter semantic steps. We are building prototypes and will use simulations to show that our approach scales, verifying that those early steps reduce the data set sufficiently to make the application of semantic approaches feasible. Semantic annotation in step *iv)* of Fig. 2 is unlikely to be a performance bottleneck but identifying an efficient semantic mapper and reasoner for change inference in steps *v)* and *vi)* is crucial if our approach is to scale.

Session shaping uses the semantically modelled changes in service aspects over time to shape multimedia streaming services. Initially, we assume that service aspects may be independently optimized; in future work we will look at optimization over different service aspects. We propose to use rule-based optimization, with a rule set composed for each service aspect in question. When we have a sufficiently large set of rules, we will look at generalizing that rule set over many service aspects. Initially, we will apply the rule set directly to the semantically modelled changes. If it proves to be to be too complex to identify trends directly, we will investigate the use of statistical methods or machine learning to deduce trends.

Acknowledgments

The authors acknowledge the partial support of Science Foundation Ireland under the FAME Strategic Research Cluster (Grant No. 08/SRC/I1403) for the work described in this paper.

The authors would also like to thank Gabriel Hogan and Piotr Stasiewski at Ericsson for their support with this work.

References

1. TM Forum: GB929, Telecom Application Map (TAM), Release 3.2 (May 2010)
2. Kephart, J.O., Chess, D.M.: The vision of autonomic computing. IEEE Computer Magazine (January 2003)
3. Sheth, A., Henson, C., Sahoo, S.S.: Semantic sensor web. IEEE Internet Computing, 78–83 (2008)
4. O'Sullivan, D., Wade, V., Lewis, D.: Understanding as we roam. IEEE Internet Computing, 26–33 (2007)
5. TM Forum: GB922, Information Framework (SID), Release 8.1 (March 2010)
6. TM Forum: GB921, Business Process Framework Suite (eTOM), Release 8.1 (March 2010)
7. Yamagishi, K., Hayashi, T.: Parametric packet-layer model for monitoring video quality of iptv services. In: IEEE International Conference on Communications, vol. 19 (2008)
8. ITU-T: Itu-t g.109: Definition of categories of speech transmission quality (1999)
9. ITU-T: Itu-t g.1080: Quality of experience requirements for iptv services (2008)
10. Bhushan, B., Hall, J., Kurtansky, P., Stiller, B.: Operations support system for end-to-end qos reporting and sla violation monitoring in mobile services environment. Quality of Service in the Emerging Networking Panorama, 378–387 (2004)
11. ITU-T: Itu-t g.107: The e-model: a computational model for use in transmission planning (2008)

12. TM Forum: GB917, SLA Management Handbook, Release 3.0 (May 2010)
13. Toktar, E., Pujolle, G., Jamhour, E., Penna, M., Fonseca, M.: An xml model for sla definition with key indicators. IP Operations and Management, 196–199
14. IBM Tivoli Netcool Service Quality Manager
15. HP Openview Service Quality Manager
16. Ericsson Network IQ
17. Batteram, H., Damm, G., Mukhopadhyay, A., Philippart, L., Odysseos, R., Urrutia-Valdés, C.: Delivering quality of experience in multimedia networks. Bell Labs Technical Journal 15(1), 175–193 (2010)
18. Kim, D., Lim, H., Yoo, J., Kim, S.: Experience in developing a prototype for wibro service quality management system. Management Enabling the Future Internet for Changing Business and New Computing Services, 241–250 (2009)
19. Choi, J., Kwak, S.H., Lim, M.J., Chae, T., Shim, B.K., Yoo, J.H.: Service traffic management system for multiservice ip networks: lessons learned and applications. IEEE Communications Magazine 48(4), 58–65 (2010)
20. Berkhin, P.: A survey of clustering data mining techniques. Grouping Multidimensional Data, 25–71 (2006)
21. Ester, M., Kriegel, H., Sander, J., Xu, X.: A density-based algorithm for discovering clusters in large spatial databases with noise. In: Proc. KDD, vol. 96, pp. 226–231 (1996)

The Design of a Quality of Experience Model for Providing High Quality Multimedia Services

Arum Kwon[1], Joon-Myung Kang[1], Sin-seok Seo[1], Sung-Su Kim[1],
Jae Yoon Chung[1], John Strassner[2], and James Won-Ki Hong[2]

[1] Dept. of Computer Science and Engineering
[2] Division of IT Convergence Engineering
Pohang University of Science and Technology (POSTECH), Korea
{arumk,eliot,sesise,kiss,dejavu94,johns,jwkhong}@postech.ac.kr

Abstract. In the last decade, networks have evolved from simple data packet forwarding to platforms that support complex multimedia services, such as network-based personal video recording and broadcast TV. Each of these services has significant quality demands: they are very sensitive to packet loss and jitter, and require a substantial amount of bandwidth. As the quality perceived by the end user gives the most accurate view on the streamed service quality, operators are increasing their focus on this type of metric, commonly described as Quality of Experience. This paper presents the design of a Quality of Experience information model that defines important metrics for measuring service quality. Based on these metrics, we define a novel control loop that represents the relationships among Quality of Experience, the Customer, and network services.

Keywords: Quality of Experience, Multimedia Service, Information Modeling.

1 Introduction

The Internet is now supporting advanced multimedia services such as Internet Protocol Television (IPTV), Video on Demand (VoD), and Voice over IP (VoIP). In addition, network convergence encourages network architecture designs that support different types of network services in a single network. However, such services require high bandwidth and strict service performance due to transferring real-time video and voice data. Furthermore, the concept of Quality of Experience (QoE), which represents a subjective measure of a customer's experiences for services, is attracting more formalized and growing attention [1].

In this paper, we propose a QoE model for managing the quality of multimedia services perceived by customers. This model defines appropriate QoE metrics and their relationship with performance indicators and consumers, and is based on the DEN-ng information model [2]. We also present a control loop to optimize the quality of services based on the measured QoE among networks, end-users and service providers.

The remainder of this paper is organized as follows. Section 2 describes performance indicators for QoE, the DEN-ng information model and previous work on QoE modeling as related work. Section 3 presents our proposed QoE model with a control loop. Finally, conclusions are drawn and future work is discussed in Section 4.

R. Brennan, J. Fleck II, and S. van der Meer (Eds.): MACE 2010, LNCS 6473, pp. 24–36, 2010.
© Springer-Verlag Berlin Heidelberg 2010

2 Related Work

In this section, we review performance indicators for QoE, and then explore previous work on QoE modeling. Finally, we briefly introduce the DEN-ng model to set the stage for explaining our extensions to it.

2.1 Performance Indicators

The ITU-T proposed objective and subjective QoE definitions [3]. The former defines Quality of Service (QoS) delivered to the user in terms of measurable service, network, and application performance metrics, while the latter models the quality as perceived by a human in terms of emotions, service billing, and experience. The DSL Forum classified video quality metrics into three layers: service layer, application layer, and transport layer [4]. They suggested guidelines to achieve satisfactory QoE for various services. ATIS classified IPTV QoS into application and network QoS [5]. The application QoS is divided into three quality layers: transaction quality, content quality, and media stream quality. The network QoS contains the transmission quality layer. They also represented the relationships between quality layers, QoS parameters, and QoE indicators. Each layer's quality is represented by QoS parameters, and can be defined as a set of QoE indicators. The Telecommunication Management Forum (TMForum) proposed Key Performance Indicators (KPIs) and Key Quality Indicators (KQIs) for managing service quality [6]. KPIs are quantifiable measurements that reflect the critical successful or unsuccessful factors of a particular resource or service. KQIs provide an indicator for a specific performance aspect of the product or product components (e.g., service or service elements), and draw their data from a number of sources including KPIs. In [7], Korea Telecom (KT) defined relationships between KQIs, KPIs, and Customer Quality Indicators (CQIs). CQIs are quality indicators that are experienced and perceived by customers. A CQI includes metrics for service billing and customer support as well as delivered services such as IPTV or VoIP. KT defined KQIs as the QoS parameters that make up a CQI and KPIs as the metrics that make up a KQI. KQIs are mapped to a CQI and can be computed from several KPIs.

We designed our model to be compatible with the above definitions. The value of our model is that it can serve as a unifying metaphor for combining these different efforts as well as a foundation for defining new functionality. We have focused on the subjective QoE part of the ITU-T QoE definition, but the human factors such as emotions are excluded from our model at this time; this is part of our future work. We use ATIS quality layers to model different kinds of QoE traffic. To model the metrics of QoE, we use enhanced versions of the KQI and the KPI concepts of the TMForum, and enhance the CQI concept of KT. Based on the CQI concept of KT, we propose a Consumer Role Quality Indicator (CRQI) that is related to ConsumerRole in DEN-ng. This builds on the concepts of KT's CQI, but applies them to different consumer, user, and administrator *roles*.

2.2 QoE Modeling

In [8], an autonomic management architecture was proposed to optimize the QoE in multimedia access networks. Their main design goals are to provide a scalable generic design that can support autonomic behavior. In their architecture, a Monitor Plane monitors the network and builds up knowledge about a network, a Knowledge Plane analyzes the knowledge and determines the ideal QoE actions, and an Action Plane enforces these actions in the network. The proposed architecture was validated by simulation.   In [9], the authors presented a Web Ontology Language (OWL)/Semantic Web Rule Language (SWRL) based knowledge base that can be used in an autonomous QoE management architecture for the access network. In their architecture, some SWRL rules can detect QoE drops. In addition, the ontology can be used to enable autonomic behaviors, where the right configuration of QoE optimizing actions is computed using SWRL rules. In [10], the authors presented an algorithm that predicts the QoE of progressive download services in real-time. The algorithm only depends on the flow of TCP data and acknowledgement packets. They do not require additional feedback from the client. To our best knowledge, none of the previous QoE models considered a control loop that includes the combination of a consumer, a service provider, and measured QoE data. Through our proposed control loop, we can detect Service Level Agreement (SLA) violations and change network configurations to provide contracted QoE.

2.3 DEN-ng Information Modeling

The DEN-ng [2] is an object-oriented information model that describes different entities of interest in the managed environment. We use it to build a technology-neutral information model (i.e., a model that is independent of technology, platform, and protocol) describing important concepts and mechanisms to represent, measure, and manage QoE. The existing QoE model in DEN-ng will be described in Section 3. The DEN-ng model uses software patterns [11] to more efficiently describe complex architectures and make the model more understandable and extensible. A pattern defines a generic, reusable solution to a commonly occurring problem. When we design a model, we can improve our model's readability by defining software patterns and repeatedly using them in solving similar problems. Two common patterns are the composite pattern [11] and the role-object pattern [12]. The composite pattern is used to define bundles, groupings, and other hierarchical and network-oriented structures that represent part-whole hierarchies. The role-object pattern enables a component object to be adapted to different needs through transparently attached role objects. This pattern is especially useful in separating the intrinsic and contextual characteristics and behavior of an entity. A person is thus modeled as an object that can have multiple roles attached; each role defines different responsibilities and functions of that person. This avoids the trap of altering the definition of a person due to changing responsibilities. The role-object pattern is also useful for other types of entities, and is used extensively in the DEN-ng model.

The policy pattern [2] is an example of a novel DEN-ng pattern. It provides policy-based management governance. In this pattern, policy rules are used to determine the characteristics and behavior of an association using an association class. The association class represents the semantics of a relationship as a class, which enables the relationship to have a set of associated attributes, relationships, and other model elements as required. The attributes (and possibly additional relationships) of the association class are then modified by the policy rules. In DEN-ng, this enables changing context to select new applicable policy rules, which then change the attributes and/or relationships of the selected association accordingly.

3   Proposed QoE Model

This section examines the QoE model in the current DEN-ng model and identifies changes required to better manage the QoE of managed, contracted services.

3.1   The Original DEN-ng QoE Model

Fig. 1 shows the QoE model in DEN-ng. The ResourceFacingService class represents services that are required to support a service that is provided to a customer, but is not visible by that customer. The programming of a QoSService is represented in DEN-ng as a set of NetworkForwardingServices. For example, during the forwarding process, packets can be queued or dropped.

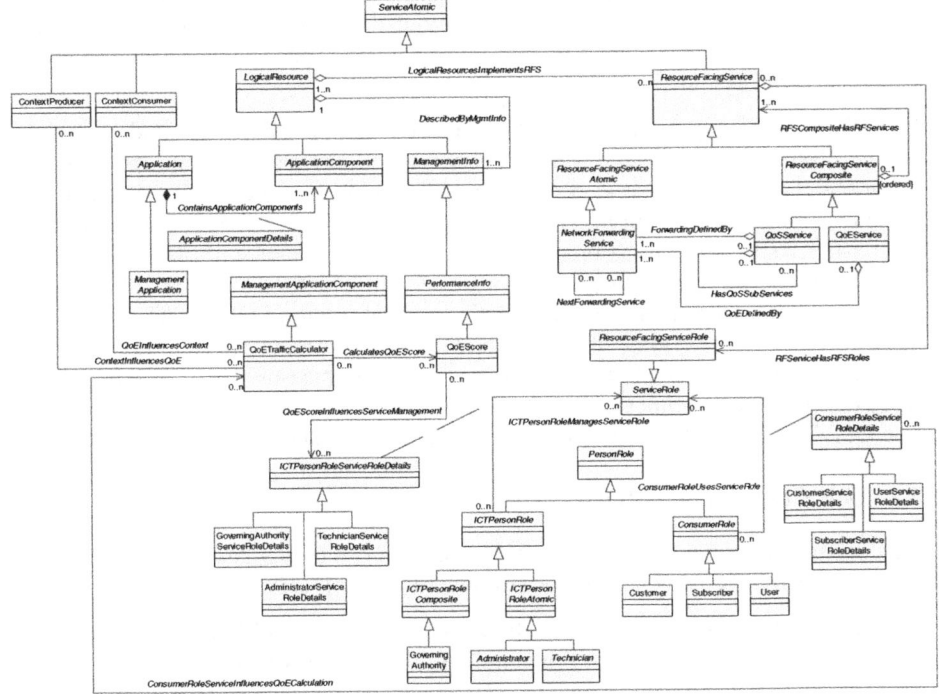

Fig. 1. DEN-ng QoE Model

QoE related classes. The DEN-ng model has three main classes for representing QoE concepts: QoEService, QoEScore, and QoETrafficCalculator. The QoEService class is defined as a type of ResourceFacingServiceComposite, because it can use one or more ResourceFacingServices to define and measure the quality of the traffic as experienced by the end user. QoEService is a generic specification for defining the different types of sub-Services that are required to implement a specific type of QoS used to provide the contracted QoE. This enables business rules to be mapped to the network, and define services that the network provides. The QoETrafficCalculator calculates the QoEScore, which defines the value of the QoE for a particular type of traffic in a given Context. The QoEScore class represents the calculation of the QoE for a particular type of traffic in a given Context. The QoETrafficCalculation class models the calculation of QoE for a particular type of traffic. The overall context in which this traffic exists, as defined by the ContextInfluencesQoE association, can affect the types of calculations performed.

The first problem with the QoETrafficCalculation class is that it has no subclass. As we mentioned in Section 2, the QoE can be divided into several types of QoEs, each of which represents the perceived quality about a specific aspect of the service. So, the QoETrafficCalculation class should have subclasses for calculating the QoE for each service aspect. The second problem is that there is no metric for defining or measuring the QoE. In the DEN-ng model, there is a class that represents the performance information of a service, PerformanceInfo. The PerformanceInfo has two classes for representing the quality of the network services: the KQI and the KPI. To indicate the QoE, a new class for representing the perceived quality is needed. In addition to that, the KQI and KPI classes should be refined to represent a more detailed and clear meaning.

Overall relationship between the QoE related classes. DEN-ng models the QoE related classes and the relationships between them. We can calculate the QoEScore using QoETrafficCalculator as a function of the context of the traffic service and the consumer related information. The calculated QoEScore influences the management of consumer services; this is modeled by relating the ICTPersonRole that represents the role of a person who manages the traffic service with the QoEScore. In the current DEN-ng model, there is no explicit relationship between a QoE model and an SLA. This prevents the checking of SLA violations and defining appropriate changes to manage services to provide better QoE based on the measured QoE. Thus, relationships between the existing QoE model and classes for measuring the QoE are needed. The QoETrafficCalculator can use those relationships and classes.

3.2   QoE Control Loop Model

This section describes a control loop for managing services based on the measured QoE. We explain it using a concrete example of the QoE service, a cache service.

QoE Control Loop. To provide a satisfactory QoE, a control loop that manages services based on the measured QoE is required. The QoE is a function of both the quality perceived by a consumer as well as the specific network performance provided by a service provider. Therefore, the control loop should include a network, a consumer, and a service provider, as shown in Fig. 2.

Fig. 3 shows how the control loop in Fig. 2 is designed in the DEN-ng model. The QoETrafficCalculator and the QoEServiceFeedback comprise the QoEControl part. The QoETrafficCalculator calculates the QoEScore, which represents the calculated QoE; the QoEServiceFeedback monitors the SLA (which is a subclass of ContractualAgreement) and makes changes to the NetworkForwardingServices as required in order to ensure that the SLA is not violated. The ContractualAgreement represents the SLA part. The ContractualAgreement represents agreements that have contractual

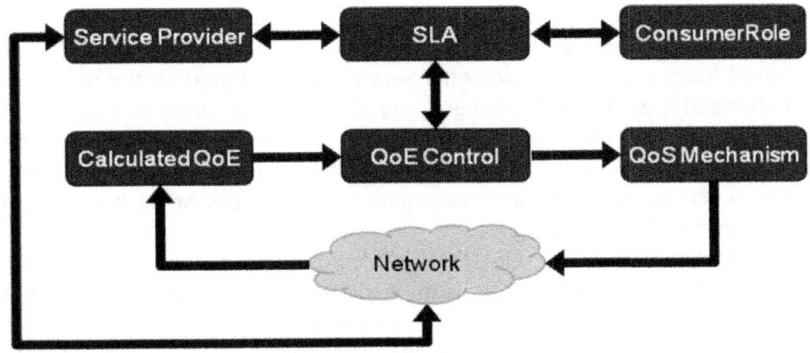

Fig. 2. QoE Control Loop - High-Level View

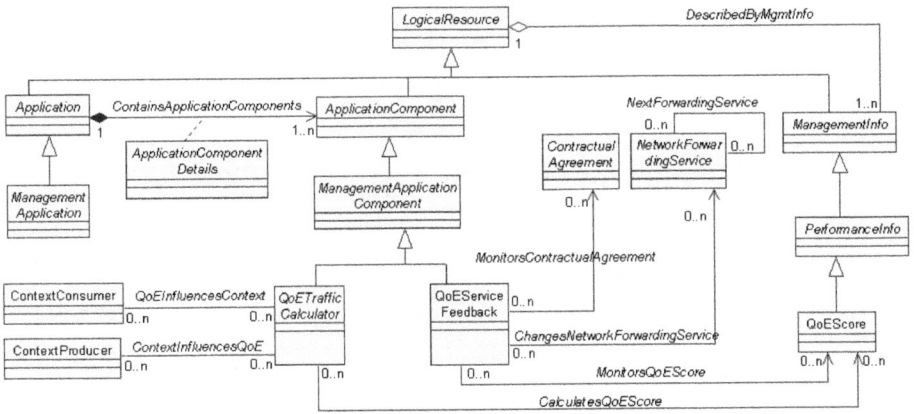

Fig. 3. QoE Control Loop - Model View

obligations, along with optional compliance and violation conditions. The ICTPersonRole (in Fig. 1) represents the different people or groups of people that manage network devices, while the ConsumerRole part represents three different types of people (Customers, Subscribers, and Users) that have different relationships with Service Providers (specifically, they represent the roles of buying/receiving, ordering and/or subscribing to, and using products and services, respectively). Note that both ICTPersonRole and ConsumerRole are subclasses of PersonRole. In contrast, the ServiceProvider portion of Fig. 2 is a subclass of OrganizationRole (shown in Fig. 4); both PersonRole and OrganizationRole are subclasses of PersonOrOrgRole, which is a type of Role. Hence, roles are used to describe how providers and users of services are related to an SLA.

The QoEServiceFeedback class triggers one or more changes to network device configurations according to management policy when any SLA violation is detected. The QoEServiceFeedback compares the measured QoEScore with appropriate parameters of the ContractualAgreement and changes the network service parameters to ensure compliance with the ContractualAgreement. A combination of QoE and QoS mechanisms are used for this change. The NetworkForwardingService, which has QoEService and QoSService as two of its subclasses, implements this. By using the QoE control loop, we can provide better service quality based on the measured QoE. More importantly, as the QoE changes, our QoE control loop can respond to these changes and adjust the QoS mechanisms used to ensure that the delivered QoE meets the user's expectations. Our QoE control loop, which includes the combination of a consumer, a service provider, and measured QoE data, has never been proposed in previous work on QoE modeling.

The parameters used by the QoETrafficCalculator depend on the type of the QoE. Therefore, the QoETrafficCalculator is divided into different subclasses, each targeted to a specific aspect of QoE (e.g., the transaction QoE). Also, the measurement location, the measurement method, and the calculation of the QoE are dependent on the type of the QoE.

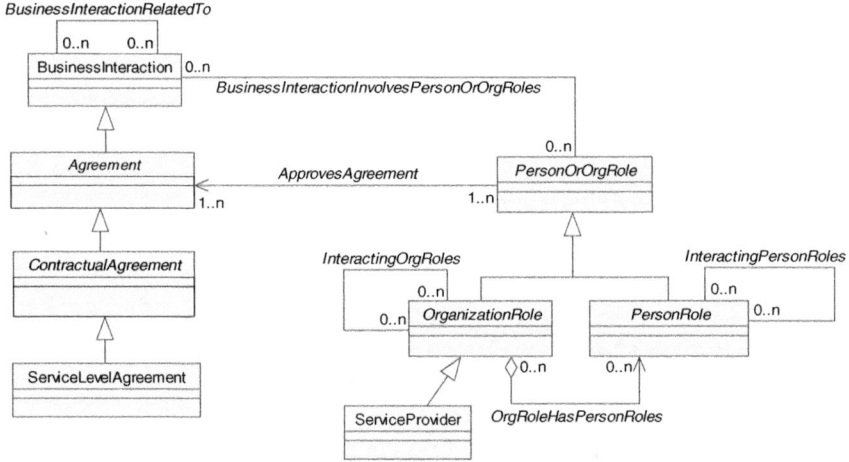

Fig. 4. OrganizationRole, PersonRole, and Agreements

We made four subclasses of the QoETrafficCalculator class based on the ATIS quality metrics: TransactionQualityCalculator, ContentQualityCalculator, MediaStreamQualityCalculator, and TransmissionQualityCalculator; these are shown in Fig. 5. The TransactionQualityCalculator and the ContentQualityCalculator calculate the QoE for customer premise equipment. The TransactionQualityCalculator calculates the quality of operations involving customer premise equipment, such as channel change delay. The ContentQualityCalculator calculates the user's satisfaction with the video and/or audio content received at the customer premise equipment. The content quality can be measured in terms of Mean Opinion Score (MOS) [13]. The MediaStreamQualityCalculator and the TransmissionQualityCalculator calculate the QoE on the physical routers in the network infrastructure. The MediaStreamQualityCalculator calculates the quality of the media stream delivered by the network. The TransmissionQualityCalculator calculates the quality of the traffic sent and received.

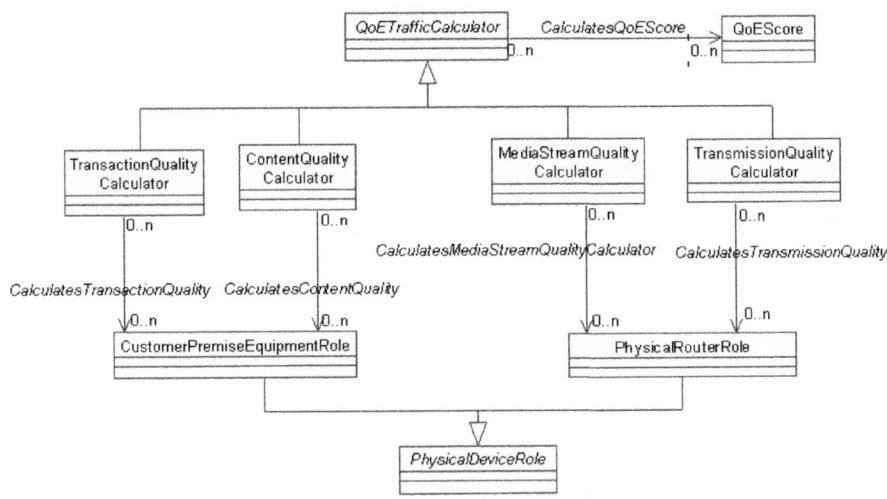

Fig. 5. QoE Traffic Calculator

Network Service for QoE. The DEN-ng model includes three kinds of traffic services to provide QoE: QoETrafficAddingService, QoETrafficModifyingService, and QoETrafficStoreAndForwardService. The QoETrafficAddingService introduces additional traffic into an existing session (e.g., Forward Error Correction (FEC) encoding). The QoETrafficModifyingService modifies the actual payload of packets (e.g., content transcoding). The QoETrafficStoreAndForwardService influences future traffic delivery based on information about the current session (e.g., caching mechanism). We model the cache service, as an example of a QoETrafficStoreAndForwardService. The cache service provides a better quality service to the user by keeping some of the data in local storage. We define a model for managing the QoE based on Cisco's Video Quality of Experience (VQE) solution [14].

The QoETrafficStoreAndForwardService is composed of three parts: the QoE traffic service component (shown in Fig. 6), the customer premises equipment component (which can be any type of device, such as a router or a modem; due to this flexibility, this component is modeled as one or more *roles*, as shown in Fig. 7), and the QoE policy management component (shown in Fig. 8).

Fig. 6 defines the high-level structure of a cache service. A cache can have a hierarchy, so we use the composite pattern to model it. The CacheServiceAtomic is divided into two classes: ContentMonitoringService and ContentDistributionService. The former provides data to the TransmissionQualityCalculator, which calculates the transmission quality using the monitoring results. The latter includes error repair and content delivery. The CDErrorRepairService specifies the cache service related error handling service. The ContentDeliveryService specifies the content delivery service between a content server and cache servers.

The customer premises equipment component deals with the measurement and the management of the QoE on the customer side. A simplified model of customer premise equipment is shown in Fig. 7; note that many classes have been elided for

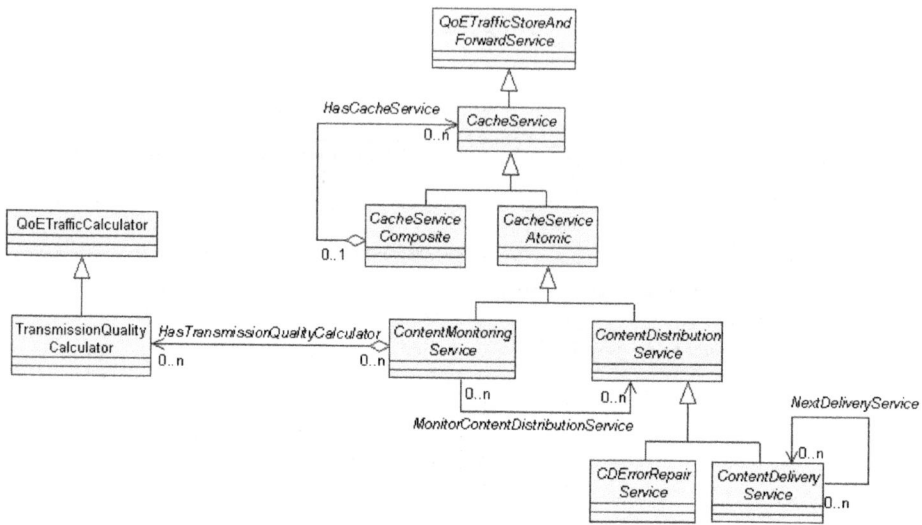

Fig. 6. QoE Traffic Service Component

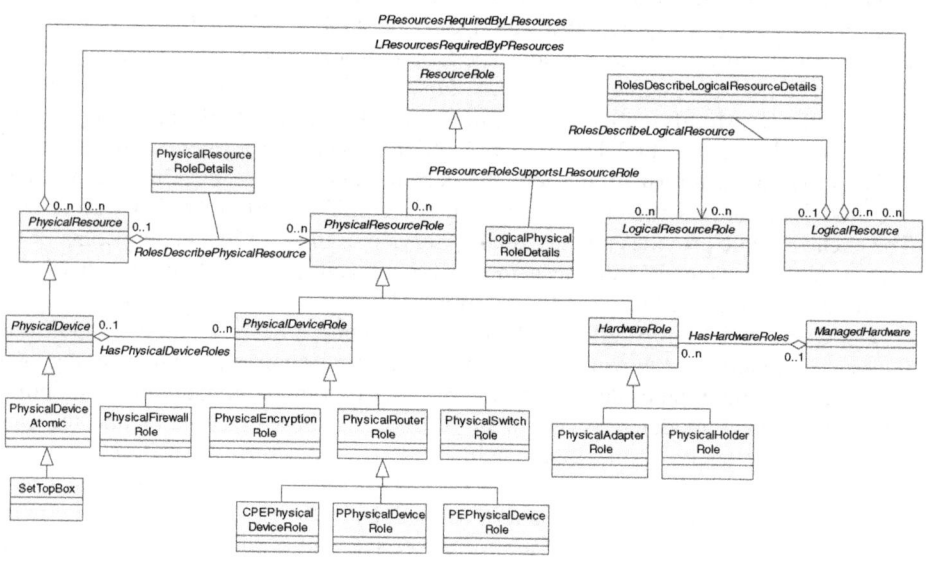

Fig. 7. The Use of Roles in Modeling CustomerPremiseEquipment

simplicity. Since a set-top box (STB) is a subclass of PhysicalDevice, it inherits the RolesDescribePhysicalResource aggregation, enabling it to take on as many roles (physical or logical) as required to model its functionality (note that LogicalResource roles have been elided for simplicity). In the case of the IPTV service, the STB is the customer premises equipment. The STB provides the interface between the customer

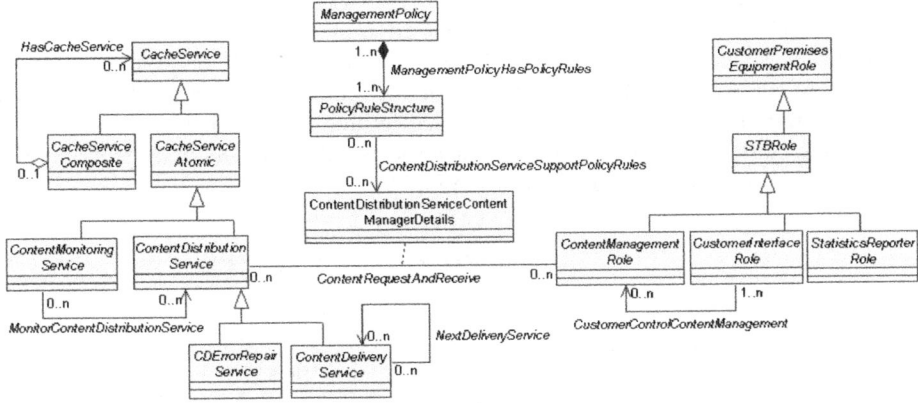

Fig. 8. QoE Management Policy Component

and the service provider. To manage the QoE on the STB, statistics about the service must be collected so that the media QoE and the transaction QoE can be calculated.

The QoE management policy component deals with the policy rules that are used to manage the quality of the service delivered to the consumer. The ContentRequestAndReceive relationship models the QoS of the content received at the STB. This relationship is dependent on both of the ContentDistributionService and the ContentManagementRole, so it is modeled as an association class whose attributes can be set by one or more policy rules (i.e., using the Policy Pattern). This represents an extensible method for managing different content based on context and role.

3.3 QoE Measurement

In this section, we introduce the QoE measurement method, and model QoE metrics using KPI, KQI, and CRQI.

Measurement methods and metrics. The DSL Forum defines three video QoE measurement methods [4]:

- *"Subjectively*, using a controlled viewing experiment and participants who grade the quality using rating scales such as MOS"
- *"Objectively*, at the service layer – using electronic test equipment to measure various aspects of the overall quality of the video signal (e.g. Peak Signal to Noise Ratio (PSNR))"
- *"Indirectly*, using measurements of network impairments (loss, delay, jitter, duration of the defect) to estimate the impact on video quality, where there is an established relationship between QoE and QoS."

The first method requires many participants using the same equipment to watch the same content. It is unrealistic, because each customer uses different kinds of equipment in different contexts. The second method needs additional equipment for measurement. Thus, the third method is the most realistic; we modeled QoE metrics based on the third method.

KPIs, KQIs, and CRQIs. In DEN-ng, KQIs and KPIs are modeled as subclasses of ManagementInfo, which is used to represent different types of management information for a ManagedEntity that is obtained in a managed environment. PerformanceInfo is a subclass of ManagementInfo, and represents various performance and other operational characteristics of ManagedEntities, Each subclass of the PerformanceInfo class defines the detailed characteristics and behaviors of a specific type of performance information. This is shown in Fig. 9.

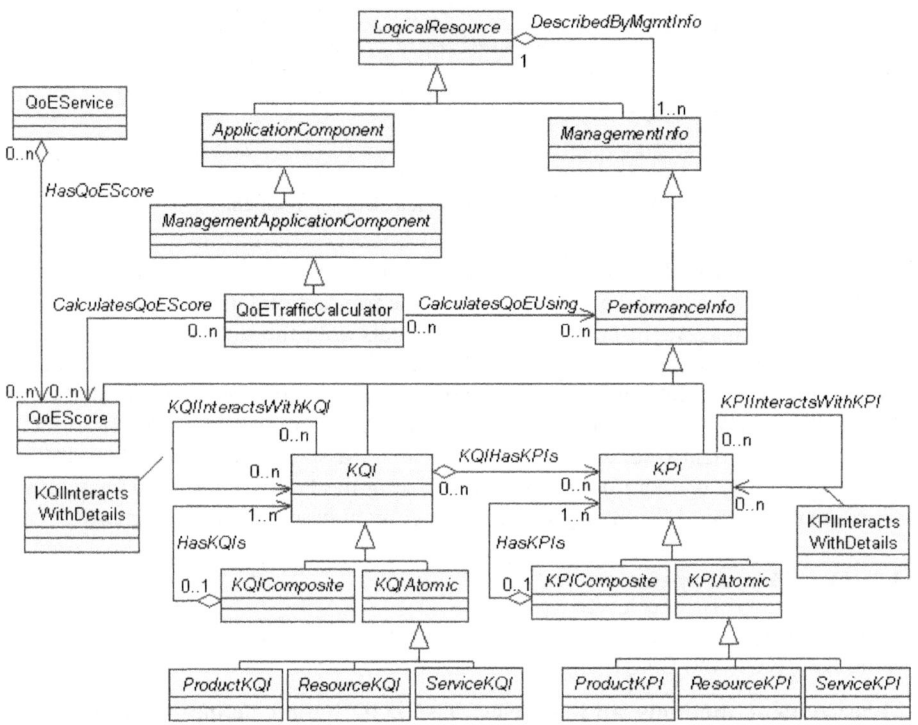

Fig. 9. Relationships among KQI, KPI, and QoEScore

We modeled KQIs and KPIs using the composite pattern. A KQIAtomic represents a KQI that can be used as a stand-alone metric, while a KQIComposite represents a measurement or a set of measurements that are made up of multiple elements (either KQIComposites and/or KQIAtomics) that are each individually manageable. The KQIAtomic is classified into three types of KQIs: ProductKQI, ServiceKQI, and ResourceKQI; KPI has similar subclasses. A KQI can contain one or more KPI(s). The relationships among KQI, KPI, and QoEScore are shown in Fig. 9.

In DEN-ng, the role-object pattern is used to model people and organizations that have different functionality. A ConsumerRole includes various types of end-user roles: Customer, Subscriber, and User. To model the relationship between the perceived quality and ConsumerRole, we define the Consumer Role Quality Indicator (CRQI) concept, which is shown in Fig. 10. The CRQI is similar to the CQI in [7];

however, the CRQI is related to ConsumerRole, and hence can model different relationships in addition to those with a customer. Since different customers have different QoE expectations, a CRQI is defined as an association class, enabling it to define different characteristics for a *pair* of ConsumerRoles and QoE data.

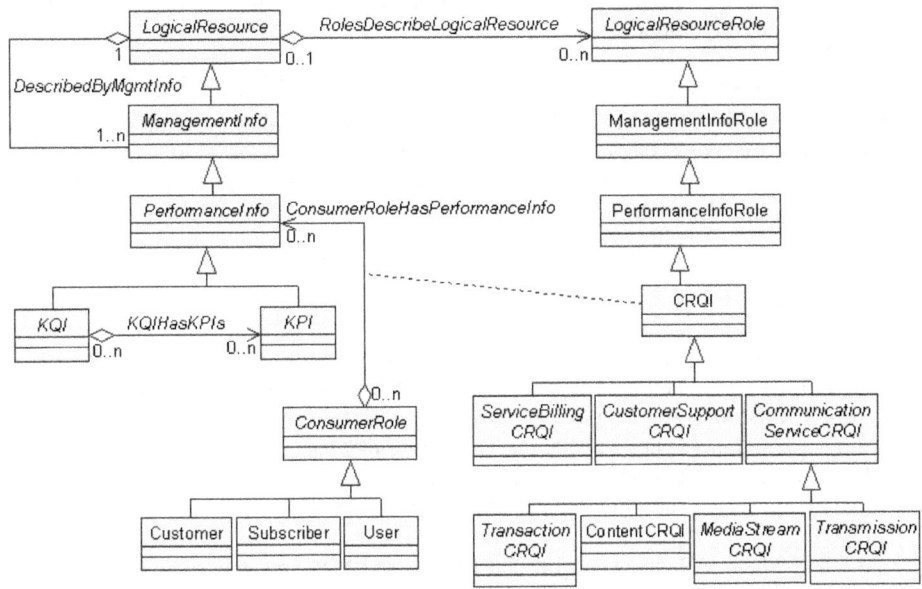

Fig. 10. Relationships among PerformanceInfo, ConsumerRole, and CRQI

A CRQI provides a measurement of a specific aspect of the quality of a product, service, or resource as perceived by a particular ConsumerRole. CRQIs can be described by a set of KQIs. Since a CRQI is defined as an association class, we can easily apply the policy pattern to it in order to explicitly represent the relationship between specific types of ConsumerRoles and PerformanceInfo. We have defined three types of CRQIs: ServiceBillingCRQI, CustomerSupportCRQI, and CommunicationServiceCRQI, which describe the perceived quality of service billing, customer support, and communication services, respectively. Note that a CRQI includes service billing and customer support aspects because they are a part of the service experience, even though they are not related to network performance. The CommunicationCRQI is based on ATIS QoE metric classification. The QoETrafficCalculator calculates a QoEScore by using these CRQIs.

4   Concluding Remarks

In this paper, we proposed a QoE model based on DEN-ng model. In our model, we proposed a QoE control loop among networks, end-users and service providers for managing services based on the measured QoE. As an example of the QoE service, we presented a design of a cache service. To model the metrics of the QoE, we extended the DEN-ng model. We proposed the CRQI that represents indicators for perceived quality. As future work, we will extend our QoE model with mapping to Management Information Bases (MIB). And then, we will develop an autonomic SLA management system using ontologies built from our QoE model. The SLA management system's goal is detecting SLA changes by relating MIB data to SLA data. We will also extend our model to incorporate human factors components to better represent the objective features of QoE.

Acknowledgment. This work was partly supported by the IT R&D program of MKE/KEIT [KI003594, Novel Study on Highly Manageable Network and Service Architecture for New Generation] and WCU (World Class University) program through the National Research Foundation of Korea funded by the Ministry of Education, Science and Technology (Project No. R31-2008-000-10100-0)

References

1. Khirman, S., Henriksen, P.: Relationship between Quality-of-Service and Quality-of-Experience for Public Internet Service. In: 3rd Workshop on Passive and Active Measurement (PAM 2002), Fort Collins, Colorado, USA (2002)
2. Strassner, J.: Introduction to DEN-ng, Tutorial for FP7 PanLab II Project (2009)
3. ITU-T REC. G.1080: Quality of experience requirements for IPTV services (2008)
4. DSL Forum TR-126: Triple-play Services Quality of Experience (QoE) Requirements (2006)
5. ATIS-0800004: A Framework for QoS Metrics and Measurements supporting IPTV Services (2006)
6. TM Forum GB923: Wireless service measurement Handbook (2004)
7. Lee, S., Im, H., Yu, J.: Analysis of IPTV Service Models for Performance Management based on QoE. In: Korean Network Operations and Management Conference (KNOM 2008), Changwon, Korea (2008) (in Korean)
8. Latré, S., et al.: An autonomic architecture for optimizing QoE in multimedia access networks. Computer Networks 53(10), 1587–1602 (2009)
9. Simoens, P., et al.: Design of an Autonomic QoE Reasoner for Improving Access Network Performance. In: 4th International Conference on Autonomic and Autonomous Systems (ICAS 2008), pp. 233–240 (2008)
10. Latré, S., et al.: Design for a generic knowledge base for autonomic QoE optimization in multimedia access networks. In: Second IEEE Workshop on Autonomic Communications for Network Management, ACNM 2008 (2008)
11. Gamma, E., Helm, R., Vlissides, J.: Design Patterns-Elements of Reusable Object-Oriented Software. Addison-Wesley, Reading (2000)
12. Bäumer, D., Riehle, D., Siberski, W., Wulf, M.: Role Object Pattern. In: PLoP 1997. Technical Report WUCS-97-34. Dept. of Computer Science, Washington University (1997)
13. ITU-T REC. P.800: Methods for subjective determination of transmission quality (1996)
14. Cisco white paper: Delivering Video Quality in Your IPTV Deployment (2006)

An Ontology-Driven Semantic Bus
for Autonomic Communication Elements

Jeroen Famaey[1,*], Steven Latré[1,**], John Strassner[2], and Filip De Turck[1]

[1] Ghent University – IBBT, Department of Information Technology,
Gaston Crommenlaan 8/201, B-9050, Gent, Belgium
jeroen.famaey@intec.ugent.be
[2] Division of IT Convergence Engineering
Pohang University of Science and Technology, Pohang, Korea

Abstract. Recently, autonomics have been proposed as a solution to tackle the ever-increasing management complexity of large-scale computing and communications infrastructures. Over time, the control loops used to orchestrate the intelligent behaviour of autonomic management architectures have evolved from fully static to highly-dynamic loops comprised of loosely coupled management components. Communication and other interactions between these components is facilitated by a communications substrate. Additionally, in order to achieve truly autonomic behaviour, the interacting components need to be able to understand each other, justifying the need for semantically enriched communications. In this paper, we present a novel semantic communications bus that orchestrates interactions between the components of an autonomic control loop. It employs ontology-based reasoning in order to establish communication contracts, validate message consistency and support semantic topic subscriptions. Additionally, a prototype was designed, implemented and its performance evaluated.

Keywords: autonomic communications, autonomic elements, autonomic control loops, semantic communications bus.

1 Introduction

The booming popularity of the Internet in recent years, has caused a great increase in size, complexity and heterogeneity of communication networks. In combination with more stringent and diverse end-user and service requirements, this leads to the proliferation of management complexity of such large-scale networks. To alleviate the problems associated with managing current and future communication networks, the autonomic communication networks paradigm has been introduced [1],[2]. Its ultimate goal is to automatically adapt the network's

---

* Jeroen Famaey is funded by the Institute for the Promotion of Innovation by Science and Technology in Flanders (IWT-Vlaanderen) under grant no. 73185.

** Steven Latré is funded by the Fund for Scientific Research Flanders (FWO-Vlaanderen).

R. Brennan, J. Fleck II, and S. van der Meer (Eds.): MACE 2010, LNCS 6473, pp. 37–50, 2010.

services and resources in accordance with changes in the environment and end-user requirements [3]. Human network administrations specify high-level policies, which represent the business goals of the organisation. The autonomic network management system dynamically translates them into low-level network device configurations. Consequently, the increasing management complexity is handled by the system itself.

Since the introduction of autonomics in the computing and subsequently network communications arena, many autonomic management architectures and control loops have been devised. When first introducing the concept of Autonomic Computing, IBM proposed the MAPE control loop [4], which is a static loop consisting of four fixed components, named Monitor, Analyse, Plan and Execute. Recently, research has indicated the need for more dynamic and adaptive control loops. For example, several architectures have been designed that integrate these ideas, including CASCADAS [5] and FOCALE [6]. Dynamic control loops are necessary in order to achieve truly autonomic behaviour, as they enable the system to adapt its core functionality to changes in the environment according to policies. Both in CASCADAS and FOCALE, Autonomic Elements are composed of loosely coupled components that perform diverse functions, such as monitoring, planning, context management and learning. Together, these components form the adaptive control loops. Additionally, a substrate is needed in order to orchestrate behaviour and communication between them. In FOCALE, this idea was advanced in the form of a semantic *enterprise content bus* (ECB) [6], which is an extension of the *enterprise service bus* (ESB) [7] paradigm. In contrast to the standard ESB, the ECB can be used to orchestrate *content*, instead of merely *messages*. Therefore, it is capable of routing on the *meaning* of the message. Additionally, it is an intelligent mediator that transforms data into technology- and platform-neutral forms. Finally, the ECB supports different types of knowledge acquisition and distribution (e.g. push, pull and scheduled) and performs common processing (e.g. semantic annotation, filtering and storage) before content is delivered to components. This enables them to register interest in knowledge in a more precise fashion, thus reducing messaging overhead.

In this paper we extend these ideas and introduce a semantic bus for orchestrating communications between autonomic control loop components. Its semantics and filtering capabilities are centred around the use of ontologies [8] derived from the DEN-ng information model [9], [10]. Messages are structured using OWL [11], which facilitates ontology-based consistency checking and semantic filtering. The goal of this paper is to formulate an answer to several pertinent research questions. First, how do we model communications and other interactions between components of an autonomic control loop in a formal and semantic manner? Second, how can existing technologies and techniques be leveraged to implement such a semantic communications bus? And third, what is the impact on performance from injecting semantics into the bus?

The rest of this paper is structured as follows. Section 2 gives an overview of related work in the field of semantic publish-subscribe systems. Section 3 explains the inner workings of adaptive, bus-driven Autonomic Elements and control loops. Subsequently, Section 4 further elaborates on the specifics of the proposed semantic communications bus. Section 5 discusses the implementation details and evaluation results of the designed prototype in more detail. Finally, conclusions are discussed in Section 6.

2 Related Work

There are a number of papers that research semantically enriched communications substrates. Most research has focussed on semantic publish-subscribe systems. Although, the ECB-inspired communications substrate proposed in this paper offers a wider range of functionalities, there is still a partial overlap. Therefore, this section gives an overview of existing semantic publish-subscribe systems.

Petrovic et al. proposed a subscription (query) language suitable for filtering large numbers of RSS (Really Simple Syndication) documents [12]. The paper describes a hybrid publish-subscribe architecture that consists of publishers, subscribers, and brokers. Publishers send data to a broker, and subscribers register their interest in receiving data with the broker. A graph-based matching algorithm is used for structural and constraint matching. Publications are represented as directed graphs; node and edge labels are both typed literals, enabling them to be related using an ontology. Queries are represented as directed graph patterns. In [13], a semantic approach is described. It extends the traditional attribute-value pair-based approach with capabilities to process syntactically different, but semantically-equivalent, information, by using an ontology. The ontology can include synonyms, a taxonomy, and transformation rules to equate different terms with each other. Our work is different from both of these approaches, in that the ontology used in [12,13] is limited to RDFS hyponym/hypernym relationships, whereas our approach can use different linguistic and functional relationships. In addition, we use OWL, as opposed to RDFS, which provides greater flexibility and representation of semantics. In [14], a semantic publish/subscribe system for RSS documents is also described. While it also uses an RDF graph, it is different from [12,13] in that it uses OWL Lite and can represent both equivalent relationships as well as hyponynm/hypernym relationships. Our work is different, in that our approach can use different linguistic and functional relationships to provide more powerful semantic matching.

In [15], the DARPA Agent Markup Language (DAML) and the Ontology Inference Layer (OIL), which later merged into OWL, were used to provide semantic publish-subscribe capabilities. Matching was defined using inferencing based on description logic. Topics are defined as ontological concepts and roles. Each publisher advertises instances of one or more topic classes, and each subscriber submits a concept description, which is a class definition, as a subscription. A DAML+OIL reasoner was implemented for checking instance inferences between each subscriber class description and publisher instance description to see if they match. A drawback of this approach is that the DAML+OIL ontologies must be agreed beforehand by the subscribers and publishers. Our approach requires no such restriction, and uses more powerful inferencing. A similar approach is used by Wang et al. [16]. However, in this work, messages are represented in DAML+OIL, instead of message topics.

Skovronski & Chiu propose a semantic publish-subscribe system that uses SPARQL queries as subscriptions [17]. Published messages are represented by instances in an ontology. When a new message is published it is added to the ontology and run against all SPARQL queries (subscriptions). If the instance matches a query, the message is delivered to the associated subscriber. However, this method scales poorly with an increasing number of publishers. When 16 publishers are registered with the publish-subscribe system, processing a single message took around 16 seconds. In this paper, we aim to improve scalability significantly.

In [18], two extensions of the SIENA system are proposed. SIENA, along with other similar systems, represents each event as a set of attribute-value pairs; hence, the subscription is defined as a set of conjunctions of simple predicates on the attributes. One extension provides ontological concepts as an additional message attribute type; this enables subsumption and equivalence relationships, along with type queries and arbitrary ontological subscription filters, to be applied. The second extension provides a bag type to be used that allows bag equivalence and filtering. Both of these extensions can be viewed as extending the semantic matching capabilities of SIENA. In particular, the first extension looks at the semantics of the data and associated metadata contained in the event in addition to the contents of the event. This approach uses a set of subsumption operators (i.e., more specific (hyponyms), less specific (hypernyms), and equivalent concepts) as well as the ability to match on any ontological property, and then reasons on how subscriptions are related to published data. Our work is different in that we use a richer notion of semantic relatedness, and we are not limited to attribute-value pairs.

In [19], a semantic method for matching topics (keywords) is defined by using the WordNet lexical database. This is structured as an application built on top of the Java Messaging System broker. Their system enables queries to be expanded and matched to a taxonomy of topics, which in turn enables topics that are related to each other to be efficiently subscribed to. However, this system is limited to hyponyms and hypernyms. Our work is different in that we can use a larger variety of lexical and functional relationships.

Finally, the semantic communications bus proposed in this paper further differs from existing work. In line with the ESB principle, it supports a wider range of delivery mechanisms, such as unicast, deliver at most once and deliver at least once. Additionally, an ESB provides other functionalities, such as transformations of received information into a form more suitable for consumption by subscribers.

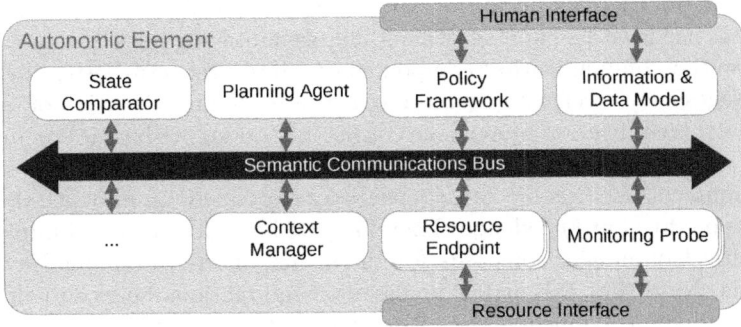

Fig. 1. Bus-driven Autonomic Element architecture

3   Bus-Driven Autonomic Elements

Bus-driven autonomic architectures discard the idea of a static control loop and introduce a more adaptive and dynamic approach to autonomic network management. In such architectures, the Autonomic Element is comprised of a set of loosely-coupled management components that all implement part of the necessary management functionality. An Autonomic Element is a self-organising management component that governs a subset of the network's resources [20]. It is capable of operating independently or collaborating with other Autonomic Elements in order to autonomously achieve higher-level goals. Each Autonomic Element exposes a specific set of management services and functionalities, which can be leveraged in order to achieve autonomic management behaviour.

Figure 1 shows an example Autonomic Element with a minimal set of management components. The functionality implemented by the example elements is roughly identical to that of the MAPE control loop [4]. However, due to the loose coupling, the ordering of components in the control loop is less strict. The advantages of this approach have been clearly demonstrated in the new FO-CALE architecture [6]. It provides a diverse set of control loops that are used in different situations. For example, some loops use the available context information to perform large-scale adjustments, while others perform more fine-grained tuning within a specific context. All of these loops use a different subset of the available management components.

Additionally, the loose coupling allows new management components to be dynamically added to or replace existing components of the Autonomic Element. This increases management modularity and makes it possible for the Autonomic Element to dynamically adapt its exposed functionality based on the environment. For example, the MAPE-like functionality as shown in Fig. 1 could be extended with new components that are capable of orchestrating federations across management domains or performing contract negotiation.

It is obvious that a communication substrate is needed to glue the management components together [6],[21]. It is responsible for orchestrating both communication and collaboration between the management components within the Autonomic Element. Additionally, in order to achieve true autonomic behaviour, it needs to be capable of handling semantically-enriched queries. This will allow the communicating components to interpret and better understand the messages they receive and send. Furthermore, the introduction of semantics facilitates the verification of message consistency, along with enabling intelligent filtering and aggregation of information. Although the need for such a Semantic Communications Bus has been repeatedly expressed, no in-depth design has been proposed to our knowledge. Therefore, we have designed and implemented a Semantic Communications Bus for intra- and inter-Autonomic-Element interactions. Note that this paper focusses on interactions between components *within* Autonomic Elements, the latter will be further studied in future work. The conceptual ideas are discussed in the following section. Subsequently, the implementation is described in Section 5.

4   Semantic Communications Bus

In order for the management components of the Autonomic Element to be able to interpret received messages, they must be enriched with semantics. This allows the management components to analyse context information and deduce appropriate action by interacting with other components. In addition, it enables the Autonomic Element to implement and maintain a dynamic knowledge base. For example, as new information is discovered, it can be semantically validated and can then be added to the knowledge base; optionally, it can be distributed to other management components within the Autonomic Element and even other Autonomic Elements that have expressed interest in updates of such knowledge. The exchange of information and other interactions are facilitated by the semantic communications bus (SCB). Messages are semantically interpreted using an *ontology*, which models management component interactions within an Autonomic Element. Gruber defined an ontology as *"a specification of a conceptualization in the context of knowledge description"* [8]. It thus describes the concepts of a certain domain, together with their attributes and relationships, in a formal manner. The rest of this section first introduces an ontology-based model for semantically representing communications and other interactions between management components. Subsequently, the core functionalities of the SCB are discussed in more detail.

4.1   Semantic Interaction Model

Figure 2 depicts the core concepts of the designed ontology. The general structure and many concepts of the ontology are modelled after the DEN-ng information model and its classes [9], [10], [22]. At the ontology's heart is the `Message` concept, which represents any type of message sent through the bus. It is the equivalent of the DEN-ng Message class and is a subclass of Event and thus Entity. Every message is sent by a single `ManagementComponent`, which is depicted by the `hasSource` property. The bus supports several communication mechanisms,

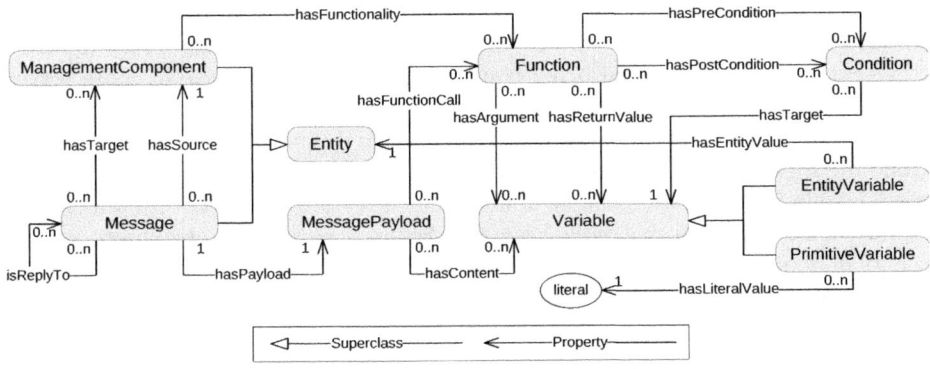

Fig. 2. The main concepts of the core ontology; sub-concepts of Entity and Condition have been omitted for clarity

such as broadcast, unicast and multicast. Therefore, the `hasTarget` property supports 0, 1 or an arbitrary number of targets. Additionally, the message has a payload which represents its content and consists of variables and/or function calls. The `Variable` concept represents information of different types, while the `Function` concept identifies function calls. The different types of variables are modelled as sub-concepts of `Variable`. The depicted ontology contains two variable types. However, new types of variables can be defined by creating sub-concepts of `Variable` or of one of its existing sub-concepts. The `EntityVariable` contains as its value an `Entity`, which comes directly from DEN-ng. It represents any type of physical or logical resource; including devices, software components, protocols, persons and even events. The `PrimitiveVariable` concept has a literal value, such as an integer, boolean or string. Function calls can be performed by sending messages with `Function` OWL individuals as payload. A function consists of an optional set of arguments, return values, preconditions and post-conditions. Every condition applies to a single variable and constrains the state of that variable before or after execution of the function call. The set of conditions associated with a OWL `Function` individual thus represents a contract that models the obligations and benefits of the function caller and callee [23]. By including them in the ontology, semantics are attached to them and the effects of a function call on the environment can be unequivocally determined by management components. This approach facilitates semantic service and functionality discovery, which will be further studied in future work.

In a bus-driven autonomic element, such as the one described in Section 3, the semantic interaction model can be used to achieve communications between the different components attached to the bus. In this case, functions are used to invoke operations on specific components, whereas messages act more as a notification system to one or multiple subscribers, where the publisher of the message does not need to know who the recipient(s) may be. In an autonomic communications scenario, typical examples of messages are those sent by a monitoring component that updates information about the resources it is monitoring or an autonomic control loop that informs everyone on the bus about the decisions it has made. Throughout the rest of this section, we provide exemplary messages that can be used by a monitoring framework that monitors one or more servers (e.g. for performing autonomic node activation [24]).

Extensibility is supported in several ways. First, the core ontology of an Autonomic Element can be extended or changed by a human administrator that is responsible for the management domain. Such a change affects all management components of the Autonomic Element. Second, specific management components may introduce their own extensions by defining new concepts or extending existing ones. These extensions are defined per message type in an accompanying ontology and are linked to the core ontology but not integrated into it. Other management components that wish to communicate with it can then take these extensions into account, while others can ignore them.

4.2   Message Type Definitions

The core ontology described above allows management components to easily define new message types. A new message type is simply a sub-concept of `Message`. For example, a message type that contains information about one or more servers in the network can be defined using description logic syntax as follows:

$$Message \sqcap hasPayload = 1 \; (MessagePayload$$
$$\sqcap \; \exists \; hasContent \; (EntityVariable \; \sqcap \; hasEntityValue = 1 \; Server))$$

What this states is that we define a new concept that must abide to two restrictions. First, it is of type `Message`. Second, it contains exactly one payload, which in turn has some content of type `EntityVariable` that contains information about exactly one `Server` entity.

Management components that connect to the SCB first register the message types they are capable of sending. These message types consist of a definition as described above and an - optional - accompanying ontology, which allows introducing new concepts in the definition (e.g. a specific type of `Server` or another type of `Message` payload next to `Function` or `Variable`) and are also added to the core ontology. The bus stores them in a repository that links each management component to a set of message types. This has several advantages. First, it allows the semantic communications bus to check the semantic validity and consistency of the message types defined by the component. Second, this set of message types represents a contract by which the management component must abide. The component implicitly agrees that it will only send messages of the types it registered with the bus. The rest of this section further explains the consistency checking of registered message types. The validation of the messages themselves is discussed in Section 4.3.

In order for a message type to be consistent and valid, it must satisfy two requirements. First, it must be a sub-concept of the `Message` concept in the core ontology (cf. Fig. 2). Second, it may not cause any inconsistencies when being added to this core ontology and the imported accompanying ontology. Both of these requirements can be checked using an ontology reasoner. The semantic bus performs several actions when validating the consistency of new message types. First, it creates a copy of the core ontology specifically for the newly registered management component. This prevents inconsistencies from arising between message types of different management components. Second, the message types defined by the management component are added to the ontology. Third, the reasoner is asked to classify the ontology. The SCB supports message type versioning to avoid inconsistencies caused by earlier versions: the versioning system ensures that only the most recent message type and accompanying ontology are added to the core ontology. If the classification process detects any inconsistencies the registration failed, and the component is not allowed to use the bus. Finally, the bus checks if all defined message types are classified as sub-concepts of **Message**. If this is not the case, the registration process fails as well. Otherwise, the registration is successful and the management component can start using the bus.

Clearly, the algorithm described above is time-consuming, as the core ontology is copied, all defined message types are added to it, and the entire ontology is classified. However, this process only occurs when a new management component is plugged into the Autonomic Element. This only occurs rarely, so the execution time is of lesser importance.

4.3   Message Instantiation and Validation

Management components can send messages onto the bus by creating OWL individuals that are members of the message types defined by the source component when it registered with the SCB. The SCB validates this by classifying any sent messages and checking their membership with the defined message types. If the created OWL individual is a member of at least one message type defined by the source component, it is considered valid and the SCB forwards it. Hence, this validation process consists of an ontology reasoner performing realization reasoning, which checks if the OWL individual belongs to a specific class. As this can be a time-consuming step, the SCB allows to turn the message validation off.

As an example, we define an OWL individual of the message type shown in Section 4.2. The message and its payload can be created as follows:

$$m : Message \qquad p : MessagePayload \qquad v : EntityVariable \qquad s : Server$$
$$(s, \text{``}10.10.0.1\text{''}) : hasIPAddress \qquad (v, s) : hasEntityValue$$
$$(p, v) : hasContent \qquad (m, p) : hasPayload$$

4.4   Subscription

As is the case with classic publish-subscribe mechanisms, our semantic communications bus supports the use of subscriptions. By registering a subscription, a management component indicates interest in specific messages. All messages that belong to a message type to which a component subscribed are delivered to it. However, in contrast to classical subscription mechanisms, the SCB does not require publishers to explicitly declare the topic a message belongs to. Rather, the subscriber actually defines the structure of the message types in which it is interested. A subscription is thus specified the same way as a message type definition (cf. Section 4.2). For example, a management component can define a message type subscription stating it is interested in all messages that relate to a specific server:

$$Message \sqcap hasPayload = 1 \ (MessagePayload$$
$$\sqcap \ \exists \ hasContent \ (EntityVariable$$
$$\sqcap \ hasEntityValue = 1 \ (Server \sqcap hasIPAddress = \text{``10.10.0.1''})))$$

Note that, although this subscription is considerably different than the message type definition presented in Section 4.2, it will still match with the message of that specific type as the definition is a subset of that message type. Obviously, this approach adds a great deal of flexibility compared to the classical topic hierarchies. Now, subscriptions can relate to any part of the message, such as its content, source or targets. For example, a management component can define a message type subscription stating it is interested in all messages sent towards himself as follows:

$$Message \sqcap \ \exists \ hasTarget \ (ManagementComponent \sqcap \ hasId \ni myId)$$

This approach also makes it easy for a component to indicate interest in all messages, merely by creating a message type that is equivalent to the `Message` concept.

Obviously, a management component can indicate interest in several message types. Every message that satisfies at least one of them is admitted to the component by the bus. Checking whether or not a message satisfies a specific subscription definition is as simple as determining if it is a member of the message type defined by that subscription. This can be done in the same way as described in Section 4.3.

5   Evaluation Results

A prototype was implemented to validate the performance of the SCB. We focus on the message sending functions of the SCB. The implementation is based on OSGi, which is a Java-based, modular platform that supports at-runtime starting and stopping of software bundles. Therefore, it is highly suited for implementing the loosely-coupled interactions needed by our bus-driven autonomic architecture. The SCB itself is based on the OSGi Event Admin bundle, which is an event-driven publish-subscribe mechanism. Our implementation uses the OWLAPI[1] library for representation and the Pellet[2] library for reasoning.

The implementation, as described above, was used to measure performance of the main functions of the SCB. Performance was measured in terms of execution

---

[1] http://owlapi.sourceforge.net
[2] http://clarkparsia.com/pellet

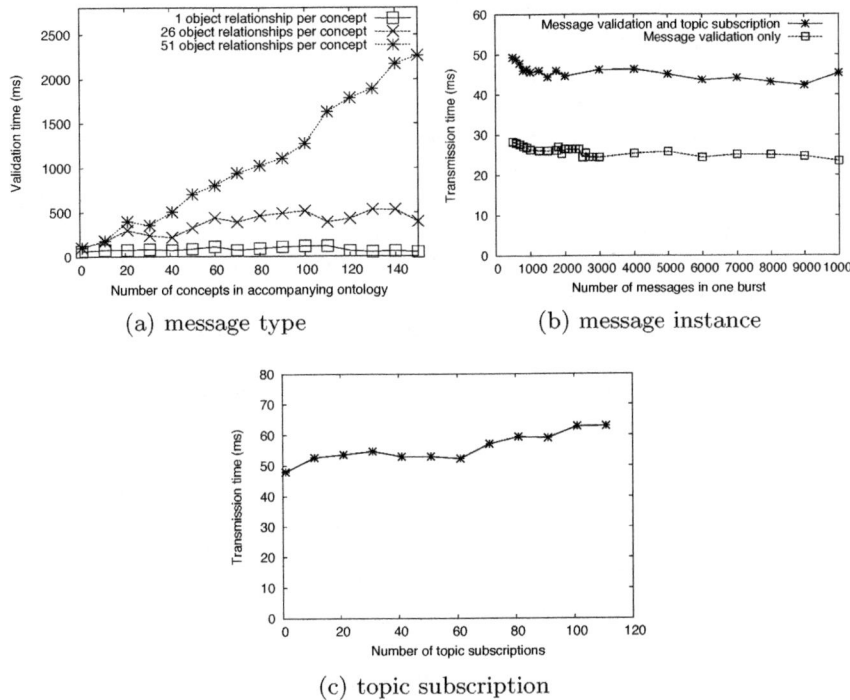

(a) message type   (b) message instance

(c) topic subscription

Fig. 3. Performance, in terms of validation and transmission time of the prototype detailed in Section 5 for an increasing message type complexity (a), message burst size (b) and number of topic subscriptions (c)

time (i.e. checking consistency and validity) or transmission time (i.e. sending messages). All tests were performed on a machine with an AMD Athlon 64 X2 Dual Core 5200+ processor with 1 GiB memory. Each test was repeated 20 times, we present average values; all standard deviation values were less than 3% when compared to the corresponding average values. Figure 3a shows the time required to validate a single message type (cf. Section 4.2) as a function of the number of concepts in the core ontology and the number of object relationships linking to each concept. For this purpose, randomly generated concepts and relationships were added to the accompanying ontology (cf. Fig. 2). Figure 3b plots the time required to send a single message as a function of the burst size, which is defined as the total number of messages sent over the SCB simultaneously. Finally, Figure 3c illustrates the impact of the number of topic subscriptions on the time needed to send a message (cf. Section 4.4).

The results depicted in Fig. 3a clearly show that the time needed to validate a message type depends on the number of property relationships in the accompanying ontology and less on the actual number of concepts. For a small number of object relationships attached to each concept, the validation time does not increase much when the number of defined concepts increases. However, even for an ontology with 150 concepts and 51 property relationships per concept the validation time is just over 2 seconds. As we do not expect the number of property relationships to grow very high and message type validation is only performed when a new component is plugged into the Autonomic Element, such execution times make it feasible to use an ontology driven message type definition.

Figure 3b shows that the time needed to transmit a message depends little on the burst size. If no topic subscriptions are defined, and consumers thus receive all messages, the transmission time converges to about 25 ms per message, which means the SCB can send about 40 messages per second. Subscribing to a topic also introduces some overhead as an additional reasoning step is needed: in this case the transmission time converges to about 45ms, which corresponds with approximately 22 messages per second. As sending a message over the default OSGi Event Admin takes only 0.04 ms, most of this delay is caused by the reasoner. The added benefit of formal validation and topic subscription, offered by the SCB, is therefore not viable for time critical applications that require the sending of hundreds of messages per second. However, we believe that the message frequency will be considerably lower in an autonomic element system, where messages are typically sent because of an update of monitor information. Furthermore, we believe this delay can be further decreased by introducing additional optimizations, such as incremental reasoning and grouping of messages.

As can be seen in Figure 3c, the number of topic subscriptions per consumer of the SCB does have an impact on the total transmission time but the increase is not high: increasing the number of topic subscriptions up to 110 only leads to an increase of transmission time of 18ms. Therefore, the SCB makes it possible to transmit messages even when consumers have subscribed to a lot of topics. In practice, the number of topic subscriptions is likely to be much lower: such a high number represents topic subscriptions that are narrowly defined. It is realistic to assume that in such a case, a consumer would opt for only a few topics, of which the subscriptions are defined more broadly.

6   Conclusion

In this paper, we presented a novel semantic communications bus (SCB) for orchtestrating interactions between loosely-coupled autonomic management components. Using an ontology, the SCB supports the exchange of semantically-enriched messages, which in turn accommodates the interpretation of exchanged information and requested functionality. Additionally, it provides mechanisms for checking the validity and consistency of these messages. Finally, autonomic components using the SCB can register interest in specific types of messages in a semantic way. Obviously, this approach achieves greater flexibility than classical publish-subscribe topic hierarchies, as it allows subscriptions to relate to any part of the message structure.

In order to validate the feasibility, applicability and performance of the designed SCB, a prototype was implemented using the OSGi platform. The implementation was used for a preliminary performance evaluation. The results show that, while performing ontology based reasoning does have an impact on performance, the additional overhead still allows sending messages quickly through the bus with transmission times between 25 and 45 ms for a first prototype. As the message validation and topic subscription algorithms focus on maintaining the accompanying ontology as small as possible, ontology reasoning times in the order of milliseconds can be achieved, which is reasonably fast for an ontological approach. Furthermore, we believe that we can further decrease these transmission times by applying more specific reasoning algorithms (e.g. incremental classification) and by grouping messages, message types and topic subscriptions.

In future work, we are planning to further optimize performance of our prototype. Additionally, the interaction model will be extended in order to support semantic interactions and contract-based collaborations not only within but also across Autonomic Element. Finally, the ontology-based function definitions will be further extended in order to achieve semantic service and functionality discovery.

Acknowledgment. We would sincerely like to thank Bert Vankeirsbilck, Pieter Simoens and Femke Ongenae for their valuable feedback and fruitful discussions.

References

1. Dobson, S., Denazis, S., Fernandez, A., Gaïti, D., Gelenbe, E., Massacci, F., Nixon, P., Saffre, F., Schmidt, N., Zambonelli, F.: A survey of autonomic communications. ACM Transactions on Autonomous and Adaptive Systems 1(2), 223–259 (2006)
2. Jennings, B., van der Meer, S., Balasubramaniam, S., Botvich, D., Foghlu, M.O., Donnelly, W., Strassner, J.: Towards autonomic management of communications networks. IEEE Communications Magazine 45(10), 112–121 (2007)
3. Agoulmine, N., Balasubramaniam, S., Botvitch, D., Strassner, J., Lehtihet, E., Donnelly, W.: Challenges for autonomic network management. In: 1st IEEE International Workshop on Modeling Autonomic Communications Environments (MACE) (2006)
4. Kephart, J., Chess, D.: The vision of autonomic computing. Computer 36(1), 41–50 (2003)
5. Baresi, L., Ferdinando, A.D., Manzalini, A., Zambonelli, F.: The cascadas framework for autonomic communications. In: Autonomic Communication (2009)
6. Strassner, J., Kim, S.-S., Hong, J.W.-K.: The design of an autonomic communication element to manage future internet services. In: Hong, C.S., Tonouchi, T., Ma, Y., Chao, C.-S. (eds.) APNOMS 2009. LNCS, vol. 5787, pp. 122–132. Springer, Heidelberg (2009)
7. Christudas, B.: Service-Oriented Java Business Integration: Enterprise Service Bus Integration Solutions for Java Developers. Packt Publishing (2008)
8. Gruber, T.: A translation approach to portable ontology specification. Knowledge Acquisition 5(2), 199–220 (1993)
9. Strassner, J.: DEN-ng: achieving business-driven network management, pp. 753–766 (2002)
10. Strassner, J., Souza, J.N., van der Meer, S., Davy, S., Barrett, K., Raymer, D., Samudrala, S.: The design of a new policy model to support ontology-driven reasoning for autonomic networking. Journal of Network Systems Management 17(1), 5–32 (2009)

11. McGuinness, D., van Harmelen, F.: OWL web ontology language overview (2004), http://www.w3.org/TR/owl-features/
12. Petrovic, M., Liu, H., Jacobsen, H.A.: G-ToPSS: fast filtering of graph-based metadata. In: Proceedings of the 14th International Conference on World Wide Web (WWW), pp. 539–547 (2005)
13. Petrovic, M., Burcea, I., Jacobsen, H.A.: S-ToPSS: semantic toronto publish/subscribe system. In: Proceedings of the 29th International Conference on Very Large Data Bases (VLDB), pp. 1101–1104 (2003)
14. Ma, J., Xu, G., Wang, J., Huang, T.: A semantic publish/subscribe system for selective dissemination of the rss documents. In: Fifth International Conference Grid and Cooperative Computing (GCC), pp. 432–439 (2006)
15. Li, H., Jiang, G.: Semantic message oriented middleware for publish/subscribe networks. In: Sensors, and Command, Control, Communications, and Intelligence (C3I) Technologies for Homeland Security and Homeland Defense III, vol. 5403, pp. 124–133 (2004)
16. Wang, J., Jin, B., Li, J.: An ontology-based publish/subscribe system. In: Proceedings of the 5th ACM/IFIP/USENIX International Conference on Middleware (Middleware), pp. 232–253 (2004)
17. Skovronski, J., Chiu, K.: An ontology-based publish-subscribe framework. In: International Conference on Information Integration and Web-Based Applications Services (2006)
18. Keeney, J., Roblek, D., Jones, D., Lewis, D., O'Sullivan, D.: Extending siena to support more expressive and flexible subscriptions. In: Proceedings of the Second International Conference on Distributed Event-Based Systems (DEBS), pp. 35–46 (2008)
19. Lien, Y.C., Wu, W.J.: A lexical database filter for efficient semantic publish/subscribe message oriented middleware. In: Second International Conference on Computer Engineering and Applications (ICCEA), pp. 154–157 (2010)
20. Hoefig, E., Wuest, B., Katalin, B., Mannella, A., Mamei, M., Nitto, E.D.: On concepts for autonomic communication elements. In: 1st IEEE International Workshop on Modeling Autonomic Communications Environments, MACE (2006)
21. Strassner, J., Won-Ki Hong, J., van der Meer, S.: The design of an autonomic element for managing emerging networks and services. In: IEEE International Conference on Ultra Modern Telecommunications, ICUMT (2009)
22. Strassner, J.: Introduction to DEN-ng (2009), http://www.autonomic-communications.org/teaching/ais/slides/0809/Introduction_to_DEN-ng_for_PII.pdf
23. van der Meer, S.: Architectural artefacts for autonomic distributed systems – contract language. In: Proceedings of the Sixth IEEE Conference and Workshops on Engineering of Autonomic and Autonomous Systems (EASe), pp. 99–108 (2009)
24. Famaey, J., Wauters, T., Turck, F., Dhoedt, B., Demeester, P.: Dynamic overlay node activation algorithms for large-scale service deployments. In: De Turck, F., Kellerer, W., Kormentzas, G. (eds.) DSOM 2008. LNCS, vol. 5273, pp. 14–27. Springer, Heidelberg (2008)

Towards a Service Delivery Based on Customer eXperience Ontology: Shift from Service to eXperience

Khalil ur Rehman Laghari, Imen Grida Ben Yahya, and Noel Crespi

Institut Telecom, Telecom SudParis, 9 Rue Charles Fourier,
Evry cedex, 91000 France
{khalil.laghari,imen.benyahia,noel.crespi}@it-sudparis.eu

Abstract. Customer eXperience is a blue print of customer requirements. In this era of heightened competition and volatile global economy, delivering services originating from diverse sources, without satisfying thorough customer experience practices may increase customer dissatisfaction, and churn rate. In order to guarantee rich customer experience, the service delivery mechanism should shift towards customer experience centric approach. This shift from service to experience brings customer in the driving seat, whose intentions and needs trigger service delivery. This paper introduces ontological model for customer experience, intended for use in run time environments by policy based management systems, to initiate and enable service delivery based on customer experience. The work presented here can have valuable implications for future studies of customer experience based service delivery approach.

Keywords: Customer eXperience, Ontology, Policy Based Management, CR&M, Service Design Solution Process.

1 Introduction

Customer eXperience, CX, is a not just a set of metrics but it's a notion that provides complete outline of customer's needs, perceptions, intentions and behaviour developed throughout the service lifecycle. It guides operators to gauge the effectiveness of their services and business landscape.

The power is not found in a straightforward collection of customer profile, customer credit information and some SLA requirements, but rather in the means and methods by which the detailed, customer experience information is gathered, analyzed and applied to improve the service delivery to customers. Therefore, knowing what to collect, how to collect it, how to integrate it and subsequently understanding how to use customer experience information for service delivery is crucial.

The ongoing research introduces a customer experience oriented service delivery approach. The Customer eXperience model is based on cognitive science and human psychological models which generates CX requirements (both qualitative and quantitive data), and this acquired model is transformed to an ontological model to enable customer experience oriented service delivery.

To address and understand this research problem, the main focus is on a following particular scenario;

R. Brennan, J. Fleck II, and S. van der Meer (Eds.): MACE 2010, LNCS 6473, pp. 51–61, 2010.
© Springer-Verlag Berlin Heidelberg 2010

If a new customer (Customer CX history and service usage records are currently unavailable to Service Provider/Operator) orders some service, then

1. How to know his customer experience requirements?
2. How to bind customer experience with his service order? And ultimately,
3. How to deliver him a service based on customer experience requirements?

These are few relevant open questions, which will be discussed in current paper to comprehend customer experience based service delivery.

The structure of this paper is as follows: In section 2, we define the customer experience and highlight its factor "usability". In section 3, we explain why we need ontology for customer experience and describe the related concepts. In section 4, we propose a Customer eXperience based Management approach with examples of Customer Order handling process, and Service design & delivery scenario. We then conclude in section 5, and briefly present challenges & future work at the end.

2   Background

2.1   Understanding Customer eXperience

The Quality of Experience (QoE) is well received term which represents the customer/user centric aspects related to services and products, unlike QoS which is a technology centric approach. International Telecommunication Union ITU-T defines QoE [1] as "The overall acceptability of an application or service, as perceived subjectively by the end-user." Recently some standardization bodies have enhanced the QoE concepts to include customer experience [2].Tele Management Forum defines CX as "… the result of the sum of observations, perceptions, thoughts and feelings arising from interactions and relationships (direct and indirect) over an interval of time between a customer and their provider(s)."[2]. Customer eXperience is normally linked to customer loyalty and it is defined in [3] as "The sum of experiences within the organization, across all touch points and across all experiential elements: presales, order and delivery process product/service experience and post-sales support."

To our understanding, "Customer eXperience is a complete assessment of customer cognitive, aesthetic and hedonic needs. It is based on customer's general attributes, his intentional and cognitive characteristics, and the tasks he intends to perform to achieve goals in certain environment". A brief description of some conceptual terms used in customer experience definition is given in Table 1 and a generalized CX model is presented in Fig.1.

This generalized CX model is based on social sciences, and particularly human psychology, and it is influenced by Theory of Planned Behavior [5].   Model is extensible with more in-depth sub classification of concepts, which is beyond the scope of this paper.

2.2   Usability Definition

To understand the customer experience based service delivery, our current work is restricted to only one customer experience factor i.e. Usability. It is defined in ISO 9241-11 standard as "Extent to which a product can be used by specified users to

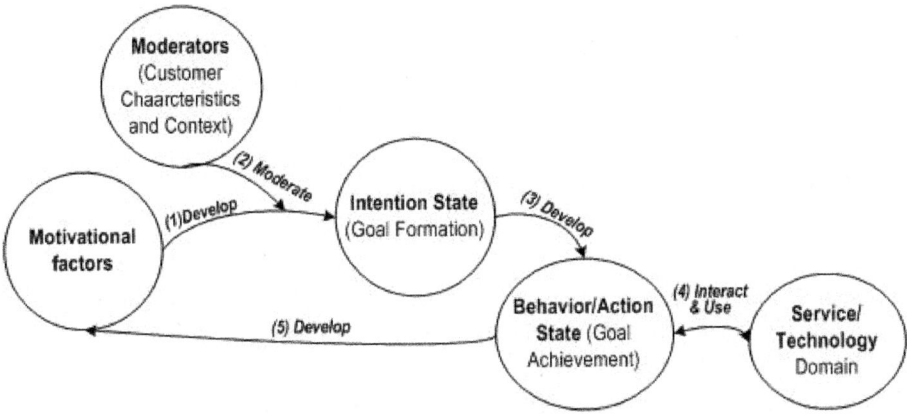

Fig. 1. General Customer eXperience Model

Table 1. Description of CX model concepts

CX Model Factors	Description
Motivational factors	It is set of factors which develop intentions, such as usefulness, usability, availability, social influences, brand image, cost etc.
Customer Attributes & Context (Moderators)	These are moderating factors posited to mediate the impact of the motivational factors on intention and behavior.
Intention(Goal Formation)	Intention is an indication of a person's readiness to perform a given behavior. [5]
Behavior/Action(Goal Achievement)	It is set of actions and related tasks triggered by intentions to achieve intended goal. During direct/indirect interaction with business entities and service usage, customers gain some negative or positive experience.
Service Domain	It represents technology and service domain.

achieve specified goals with effectiveness, efficiency and satisfaction in a specified context of use" [4]. The three core terms in usability definition could be defined as follows:

Satisfaction. It refers to the notion of Ease of Use and Joy of Use. Ease of Use refers to the learn ability and easiness to perform tasks. Joy of Use refers to the level of delight for a customer to use some service [11].

Effectiveness. It refers to the quality of the service which enables customers to achieve their targeted goals and tasks effectively. It means the completeness and accuracy with which users can achieve their goals [4].

Efficiency. It refers to the responsiveness of a system. It is actually measure of time, system takes to perform given activities, the number of steps required from the user, and the numbers of errors made during use [11].

It is important to remember that there is no single kind of user or customer, and there is also a variability of context of use. Therefore, different levels of experience, interest in the subject matter and individual needs for services should also be taken into consideration when planning a service solution based on usability factor.

3 Ontology for Customer eXperience

3.1 Motivations

In general, the application areas of ontology are collaboration, interoperation, and modelling [6]. While discussing these areas we will explain why it is relevant to have ontology for customer experience.

Collaboration and Interoperation. Ontology unifies knowledge structure which is, then, may be shared as reference for further development and participation.

Service Providers, SPs, are collaborating with more and more third parties to deliver richer services, and thus, they need to share a common understanding of customer experience factors. Furthermore, customer experience is matter of subjectivity because it represents customer's qualitative and hedonic views about services. Ontology enables interoperation of these concepts, as it provides machine-readable knowledge. Thus, having the customer experience in a machine readable format with ontology language, enable system-to-system interoperation, and hence, a dynamic adjustment of Service Providers' strategies and operations accordingly.

Moreover customer information is spread all over the information systems and in different formats; building a unified ontology for it will enable better understanding of customer and then, more revenue for SPs.

Modelling. Models for customer, service, resources and business goals are standardized, and transforming them into ontological model will enhance collaboration and interoperations in the human-to-human level and in the system-to-system level.

3.2 Customer eXperience Ontological Concepts and Use

At this stage, it's assumed that there is some Customer eXperience Model available based on some socio psychology model. Business Models are created keeping in view customer experience information. These assumed models are transformed into ontological models using ontological tools such as Protégé. The ontological model is defined through three main classes: Customer Domain, Service Domain and Business Model using Protégé. The main classes and their sibling classes are developed and all are considered disjoint. Their description is given in Table 2. The Individual (Object) properties and data properties are also created.

The ontology we developed is mainly focused on the Customer Order Handling Process, Customer eXperience Model, Service Design Solution Process and Experience based Business Model. It is developed mainly for two objectives:

1. To understand how the customer experience influences eTOM processes at CR&M and Service level, i.e., it enables matching between customer experience and CR&M and Service delivery process operations.

Table 2. Customer eXperience Concepts

Concepts	Explanation
Customer Domain	It is classified into Customer, Customer Operations and Customer Management entities, and they have more sub-classification as depicted in Fig.2. This figure depicts class view of ontology. All classes are disjoint, and the individuals (object) and date properties are defined but not visible in diagram as it is class view. The customer domain ontology is intended to provide customer experience factors and requirements at run time. It also provides interoperation. For simplicity, we have modelled only one customer experience factor "Usability" for "New Customer Order" and proposed some customer experience support operations which enrich CR&M operation set to prepare customer order as per CX requirements.
Service Domain	Service Domain Concept has also been sub-classified into service specifications, service operations, offered services and service operation management entities, and they have more sub-classifications as depicted in Fig.3. All classes are disjoint. The Service domain ontological concepts enable Policy engine to devise appropriate service plan in accordance to CX requirements. Service Design Solution develops required service features and parameters to support CX requirements.
Business Model	Business Model is presented to make better business use of rich customer experience information and trigger some interest to develop appropriate business plans accordingly which fulfil the business objectives by matching customer's true feelings. The important class in this model is Customer eXperience Business Plan (CX_BP) concept which includes some possible CX business plans as depicted in Fig.4. All classes are disjoint. Business Model ontology provides business plans based on customer experience information, likely to be differentiated on customer attributes or context information i.e. age, gender, contract, location or task wise usability requirements.

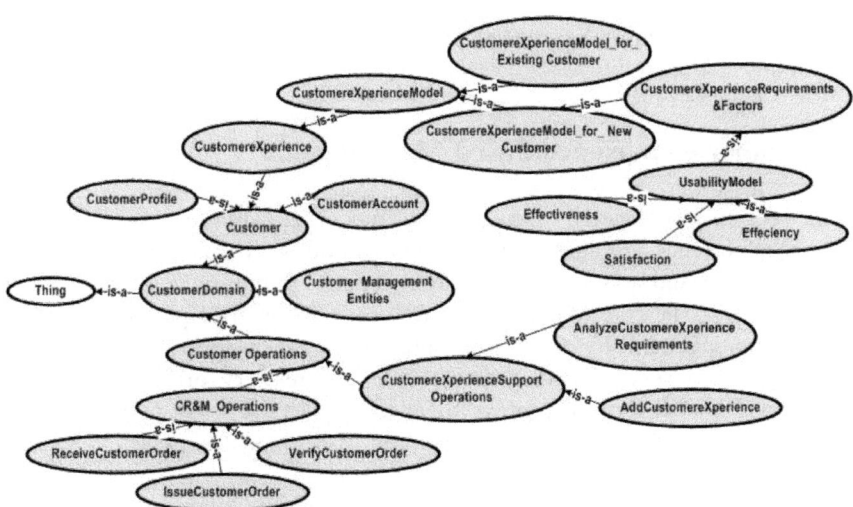

Fig. 2. Customer Domain Ontology Class View

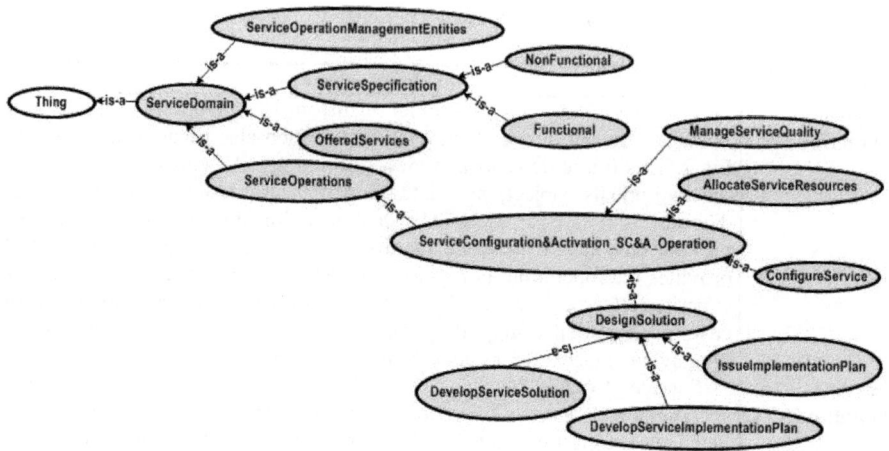

Fig. 3. Service Ontology Class View

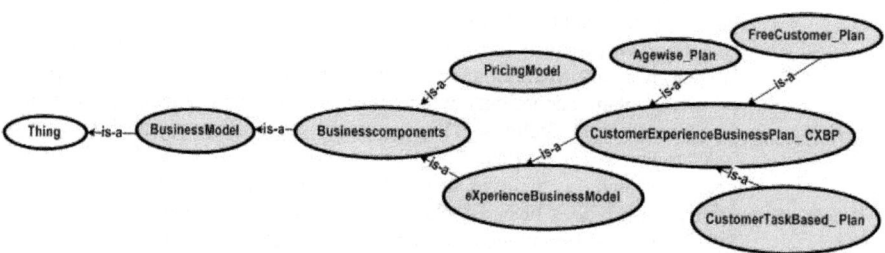

Fig. 4. Bussiness Model Ontology Class View

2. How the use of ontology enables integration and interpretation among various levels of abstraction.

4   Customer eXperience Based Management

In this section, we briefly discuss about functional architecture which enables customer experience oriented service design and delivery. Furthermore through the use of sequence and activity diagram, this concept is presented to understand this approach better. The core of our work is to bring Customer eXperience at the center of service management by employing ontology-based customer experience model, and policy-based service management. Policies are very effective for mapping customer and his/her desired context to capabilities of the set of network to support specified services. Furthermore, policies can also control service invocation and execution [7].

In the following Table 3, we introduce functional components such as Policy Engine, Knowledge Base, and Effectors;

Table 3. Description of Functional Components

Functional components	Description
Policy Engine	Policy rules have two parts condition and action, condition part describes when the action of the policy should be enforced and action part describes the features that should be enforced in case conditions are met [8]. We classify the actions of Policy Engine in two types, operations and feedback deductions. Operations are again sub classified into two parts as follows; ⇒ Customer Experience Support Operations: Actions are executed to support customer experience insertion, analysis, and activation. These operations support CR&M (Customer Relationship & Management) to enable customer experience based management. ⇒ Service Operations: Are actions directly executed on the service platform. These actions could be service design, service development, service configuration, service activation, and so forth. ⇒ Feedback-Deduction: Actions modifying the Knowledge Base by asserting new values of customer experiences or retracting existing ones.
Knowledge Base	It includes concepts and facts, as well as their relationships and the mechanisms to combine them to solve occurring problems. Ontological model is stored in KB to enable policy engine to make use of customer experience information as per appropriate policies.
Effectors	It executes rule actions to achieve desired goals.

4.1 Use of Customer eXperience and Generic Scenario

Assumptions. Customer Order (CO) is supposed to be in SAWSDL (Semantically Annotated Web Service Description Language) format in current work, but XML format could also be used. The motivation to use SAWSDL format is that the annotations normally enrich WSDL format to support semantic capabilities and non functional attributes [9]. Hence, an annotation can include customer experience factors and customer experience based business plan. The customer experience ontology is developed with Protégé and is stored in the knowledge base, which is dotted by the Policy Engine.

Hereafter, we explain how these components are interacting at CR&M (Customer Relationship & Management) level, while afterwards, a scenario is presented in Fig. 5 to illustrate how service processes should be designed and managed to support customer experience.

Customer eXperience Enriched Customer Order Handling. Here we discuss the sequence of customer order handling process where traditional customer order is updated with demands of customer experience information and related customer experience business plan. Fig.5 shows the sequence diagram for customer order management.

1. The customer consults the portal and sends a demand for the chosen service.
2. On the reception of order, CR&M issues CO (Customer Order).

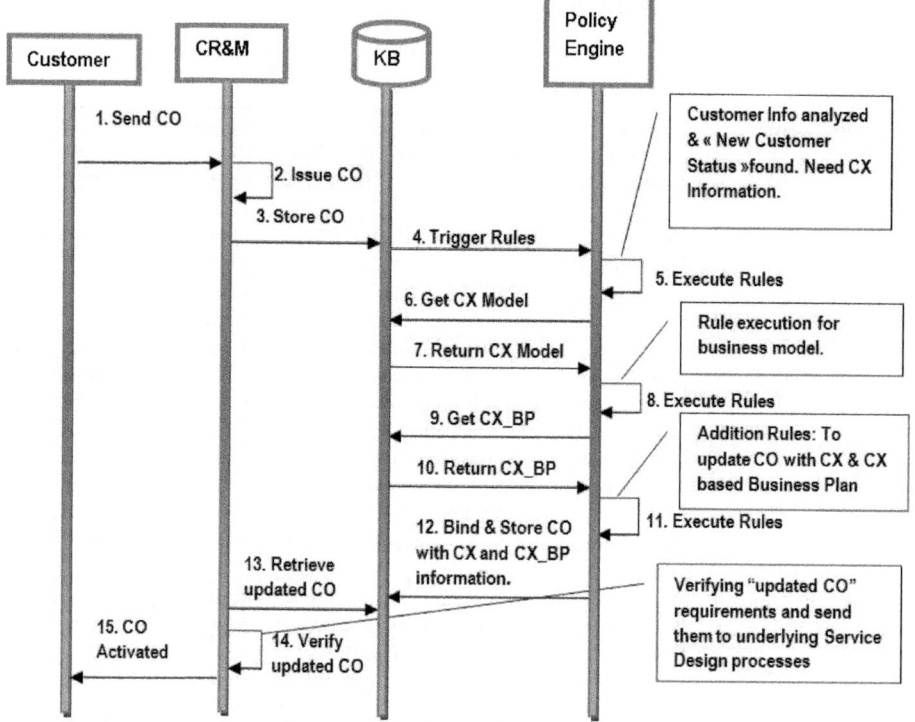

Fig. 5. Sequence Diagram: CO Management based on Customer eXperience

3. CO is stored in Knowledge Base (KB)
4. Policy Engine is alerted to trigger the related rules about Customer Order, CO.
5. Policy Engine executes appropriate rules and, we assume that this analysis shows customer status as "New Customer" and Service order demand "S". For further refinement, Policy Engine needs information about CX requirements of New Customer.
6. Policy Engine retrieves CX information from "Customer eXperience Model for New Customer" ontology in KB to add customer experience information in the customer order. For example, it finds "usability factor" requirements and retrieves concerned information from "Usability Model".
7. KB returns customer experience related information.
8. Based on CX information and Customer profile information, Policy Engine now executes rules to identify if there is any specific business plan available.
9. Policy Engine demands retrieval of the information from CX_BP "Customer eXperience Business Plan" ontology in KB to re-adjust customer experience demands (CX values/information) in the customer order as per Business Model.
10. KB returns appropriate customer specific business plan.

11. Now Policy Engine adds the customer order with the CX and Customer experience Business Plan. Thus order is updated with customer experience information and related business plan.
12. Updated CO *(UCO= CO+CX+CX_BP)* is stored in KB.
13. CR&M also retrieves updated CO.
14. It also verifies the requirements of "Updated CO" with respect to underlying Service Management & Operation (SM&O) process. Predefined rules are triggered for this updated customer order, and through the effectors, corresponding service operations are executed in order to deliver customer experience based service. This step is further discussed in next section.
15. Finally, a CO enriched with CX is activated and the customer is acknowledged.

Service Design and Delivery based on Customer eXperience. In this section, we shed light upon a key question of how to design and deliver service based on customer experience requirements. As we learnt in previous section that once the Customer Order is updated with CX, it's issued to underlying Service Management & Operation (SM&O) processes for further processing as per CX requirements. The activity diagram is presented in the following Fig.6, where we intend to show how to achieve this CX based service delivery, and we found the relevance of customer experience to the process "Design Solution" in Service Configuration and Activation (SC&A) Process. This process is described in TMF's eTOM Process Model as [10] "…The purpose of the Design Solution processes is to develop an end-to-end specific service design, which complies with a particular customer's requirement. These processes are invoked when a customer order requires special or unusual end-end service arrangements, which are not able to be satisfied using standard service arrangements". The essence of this process matches to the objectives of CX described in this paper, and thus, the realization of this process could guarantee the service design and delivery based on customer experience requirements.

1. Updated Customer Order is sent to Design Solution processes of SC&A (Service Configuration & Activation Process). In this scenario, we consider that a customer orders Service "S" and related Customer eXperience factor is "Usability".
2. In Design Solution Sub Process, first step is to build technical resources, functional and operational details of the service. The sub factors of usability such as Ease of Use and Joy of Use and service parameters like Responsiveness and Quality are to be incorporated in service solution life cycle at this stage. The Customer Centric Design (CCD) requirements related to service interfaces; websites and service features as well as service parameters (KQI) such as responsiveness and quality are also to be included during service solution development stage.
3. Once the services are designed as per customer requirements, the next step is to develop service implementation plan. It is detailed plan about how to implement service solution.

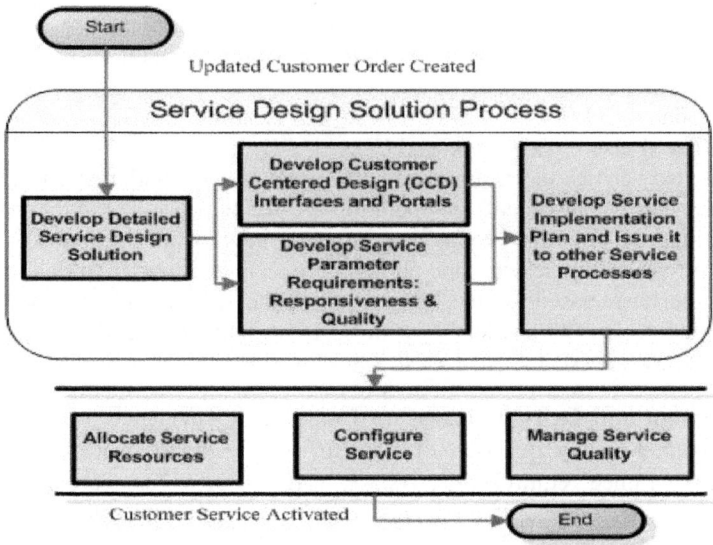

Fig. 6. Activity Diagram to demonstrate the use of Service Design processes

4. Finally the customer experience specific service features and parameters are designed and an implementation plan is issued to other related process for enabling service delivery.

From above simple scenario, it is learnt that services supporting CX could be delivered by exploiting "Design Solution" sub processes. Through detailed design solution and necessary service features development, these sub processes perform pivotal role in Customer eXperience oriented service delivery. Moreover, these processes not only invoke requests to other SC&A sub process, as shown in activity diagram, but could also invoke requests to RM&O (Resource Management & Operation) provisioning processes to determine the availability of suitable specific resources, or to suppliers /partners though the S/PRM (Supplier/Partner Relationship Management) process in the event that the service design requires either the inclusion of outsourced or partner provided specific services [10].

5   Discussion and Conclusion

This paper is in fact an introduction to Customer eXperience oriented Service delivery. To do so, the following steps are proposed:

*   Ontological Model for Customer eXperience. It integrates customer domain, service domain and business model concepts and their respective sibling concepts to prepare customer order and services in accordance with customer experience requirements.
*   Functional Architecture. The main goal of this architecture is to give an understanding of how the customer experience is refining the service delivery. And we define three main components: the Policy Engine, the Knowledge Base and Effectors. The ontological model and related policies

are stored in the Knowledge Base, while Policy Engine triggers specific policies and make use of knowledge in KB to drive CR&M and Service processes. At CR&M level, the Customer Order handling process is enriched with customer experience requirements using ontological model and policy based management. At Service level of eTOM Process framework, we focus on the "Design Solution" processes and propose a realization of CX specific service solution as well as its interaction with other processes to enable customer experience oriented service delivery.

Some of the challenges yet to be addressed are;

- Human intentions and behavioural norms are highly random in nature; it's cumbersome to precisely model human requirements.
- Service Paradigms are not so agile and adaptive to ensure service delivery based on varying customer experience requirements. However, in our future work, we intend to produce a detailed functional architecture to demonstrate the effectiveness of service delivery approach based on customer experience.

References

1. ITU-T Report 2007: Definition of Quality of Experience (QoE), International Telecommunication Union, Liaison Statement, Ref.: TD 109rev2 (PLEN/12) (January 2007)
2. TM Forum Technical Report: Managing the Quality of Customer Experience. Release 1.0 TR 148 TMF Approved Version 0.9, pp. 18 (November 2009)
3. Calhoun, J.: Driving Loyalty by managing the total customer experience. Ivey Business Journal Canada, 6 (2001)
4. ISO 9241-11 Standard: Ergonomic requirements for office work with visual display terminals (VDTs) Part 11: Guidance on Usability, ISO (1998)
5. Ajzen, I.: The theory of planned behavior. Organizational Behavior and Human Decision Processes 50, 179–211 (1991)
6. Noy, N.F., McGuinness, D.L.: Ontology Development 101: A Guide to Creating Your First Ontology'. In: Stanford Knowledge Systems Laboratory Technical Report KSL-01-05 and Stanford Medical Informatics Technical Report SMI-2001-0880 (March 2001)
7. Serrano, J.M., Serrat, J., Strassner, J., Ó Foghlú, M.: Facilitating Autonomic Management for Service Provisioning using Ontology Based Functions & Semantic Control. In: 3rd IEEE Intl. Workshop on BCN 2008, IEEE/IFIP NOMS 2008, Brazil, pp. 77–86 (2008)
8. Fahy, C., Ponce de Leon, M., van der Meer, S., et al.: Modelling Behaviour and Distribution for the Management of Next Generation Networks. In: Advanced Autonomic Networking and Communication, Whitestein Series in Software Agent Technologies and Autonomic Computing (2008)
9. Qiu, Q., Xiong, Q.: An Ontology for Semantic Web Services. In: Perrott, R., et al. (eds.) HPCC 2007. LNCS, vol. 4782, pp. 776–784. Springer, Heidelberg (2007)
10. TeleManagement Forum: Business Process Framework enhanced Telecom Operation Map (eTOM): Release 8.0, GB921Addendum D, TM Forum Approved Version 8.4 (June 11, 2009)
11. Jeng, J.: Usability Assessment of Academic Digital Libraries: Effectiveness, Efficiency, Satisfaction, and Learnability. Libri 55, 96–121 (2005); (Printed in Germany All rights reserved Copyright Saur 2005 Libri)

An Architecture for Affective Management of Systems of Adaptive Systems

Kevin Feeney, John Keeney, Rob Brennan, and Declan O'Sullivan

FAME & Knowledge and Data Engineering Group,
School of Computer Science & Statistics
Trinity College Dublin, Ireland
{kevin.feeney,john.keeney,rob.brennan,
declan.osullivan}@cs.tcd.ie

Abstract. Modern information and communications systems are increasingly composed of highly dynamic aggregations of adaptive or autonomic sub-systems. Such composed systems of adaptive systems frequently exhibit complex interaction patterns that are difficult or impossible to predict with behavioral models. This creates significant challenges for management and governance across such systems as component behavior must adapt in ways that only become apparent after the system is deployed. As a result, the complexity of modern ICT systems, such as telecommunications networks, often exceeds the technological capacity to apply coherent, integrated governance to these systems of adaptive systems. Where components are managed, they are often managed in isolation (or silos) and where intelligent adaptive components are deployed, they adapt in an isolated response to pre-defined variables in an attempt to satisfy local goals. This results in partitioned, incoherent, inflexible, inefficient and expensive management, even for locally adaptive or autonomic systems. This paper presents an approach to apply emotional (affective) modeling, and processing and reasoning techniques to the management of such a system of adaptive systems. We focus on how an emotional management substrate can ease the modeling and mapping of high-level semantic governance directives down to enforceable constraints over the adaptive elements that make up the complex managed system.

Keywords: Affective systems, management, autonomics, system of systems.

1 Introduction

As modern ICT and telecommunications systems grow, and are increasingly composed and federated together, the day-to-day management of such systems is becoming more complex. As components become more complicated it has become necessary to enable them to self-manage by embedding a degree of intelligence and self-awareness, bounded by high-level management directives – a move inspired by the autonomic nervous system [1]. However, such autonomic management approaches are based on a default assumption that the managed components must be modeled exhaustively so that their stimuli and behaviors are fully understood before

R. Brennan, J. Fleck II, and S. van der Meer (Eds.): MACE 2010, LNCS 6473, pp. 62–72, 2010.
© Springer-Verlag Berlin Heidelberg 2010

integrated control can be applied. In a large composed or federated system it is impractical to comprehensively model all future possible deployments and interactions of each constituent part so that each self-adaptive part will have a holistic view of the entire system, thereby enabling it to best constrain its own operation.

An alternative is a very agile system that can dynamically identify and reason about its environment. This implies an ability to dynamically load and predict behaviors in a way that is not supported by traditional, for example stochastic, modeling approaches. Ideally emergent intelligent behaviors would solve these problems and in many generalized or abstract use cases this may appear sufficient. However, when faced with real-world constraints and the need to demonstrate considerable advantages over traditional communications management and control systems in real time, it is unlikely that current technologies will be able to fulfill such aspirations in the immediate future.

Emotions are a higher-level cognitive means for an organism to balance competing goals and to guide decision making and enhance deliberative processing with behaviors and reactive processing to establish subjective utility values for alternative decisions and outcomes [19]. By adopting an emotional approach, a management system can be more flexible in uncertain and complex environments, can interpret constraints and provide feedback via the human governance interface in a more effective manner; can better select between goal achieving behaviors; and can operate in a more opportunistic way.

This paper presents ongoing research to develop the theoretical and engineering foundations for a new breed of intelligent management system capable of applying coherent governance across highly complex distributed, heterogeneous, adaptive systems of systems. The approach presented here is based on a hierarchical control architecture coordinated by an "affective controller" which uses an affective model and a control loop based on appraisal theory to guide sub-system behavior towards high-level governance goals. The use of techniques inspired by neuro-biological models in this domain is not new, e.g. IBM's Autonomic Systems initiative [1], however such systems are generally limited to controlling relatively well-contained sub-systems whose behaviors adapt on a small number of variables according to well-known models [2]. How such autonomic systems can be integrated into larger managed systems remains an unexplored area that our research addresses [3].

Affective models have been applied to the problem of decision making in complex environments in research domains such as multi-agent systems [4], robotics [5][6][7][8], cybernetics [9], autonomics [10][11][12], games [13], human-computer interaction (HCI) [14] and cognitive systems [15][16]. Our work extends the state of the art in affective control systems by incorporating them into a hierarchical architecture that allows intelligence to be distributed across the network. In the field of telecommunications management our work is pioneering the application of affective reasoning to the problems of integrating and coordinating adaptivity; filtering and appraising events; and enabling human governance through an innovative and intuitive interface.

The twin foci of our work are on the use of a common emotional-behavioral model to:

- facilitate effective human governance of such a system through the expression of goals and constraints that are largely decoupled from the underlying (and time-varying) complexities of the adaptive system;

- enable a new software engineering process for adaptive system design focused on a hierarchical, three tier architecture for affective-adaptive systems, that emphasizes runtime flexibility, local autonomy, the ability of higher level controllers to provoke/suppress behavior in lower layer controllers, the fusion of stimuli as they reach higher layers and the ability of higher layer controllers to influence stimuli fusion and generation in lower layers.

The rest of this paper is structured as follows: In the following sections we introduce the affective management architecture and discuss how it can be implemented. We also discuss a number of shortcomings of current autonomic approaches for managing a system of adaptive systems, and give examples of how the affective approach has been successfully applied in a number of other application domains. We then give two motivating example applications in the telecoms management domain, then we present a discussion of the applicability of the affective management approach. Finally we provide some concluding remarks.

2 Architecture

The design of the affective management system is based on a hierarchical, multi-layer controller architecture (Fig. 1). Each controller in the hierarchy implements a generic controller model, as shown in Fig. 2 and Fig. 3. The control activities at each level in the hierarchy (reactive, adaptive, affective) are as follows:

At the level of a traditional reactive controller, e.g. a sensor network gateway or a telecommunications service switching function, stimulus fusion (Fig. 3) is a simple relay of received events, the event-condition-action (ECA) policy rules define specific stimulus-response rules and the number of behaviors is limited to pre-defined management actions.

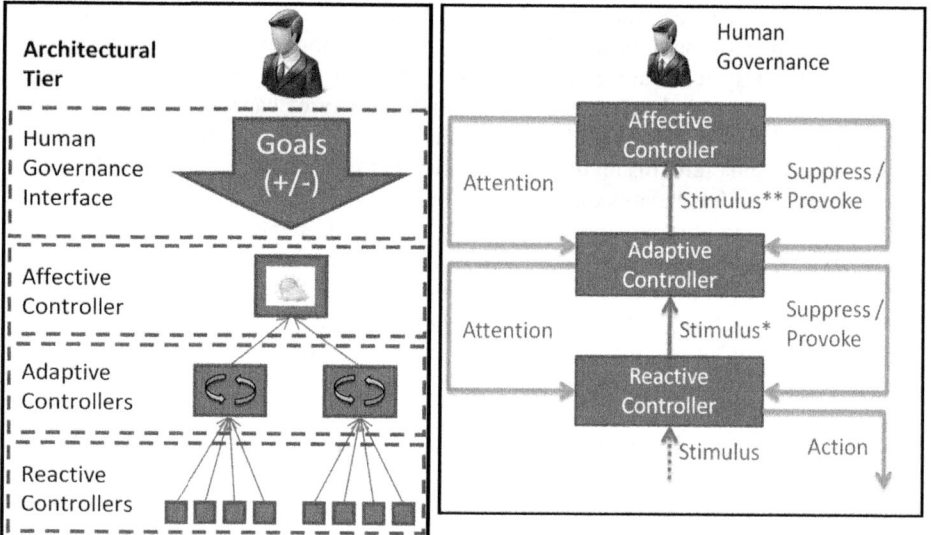

Fig. 1. Hierarchical affective management architecture Hierarchy

Fig. 2. Interactions between controllers in the a hierarchical affective management architecture

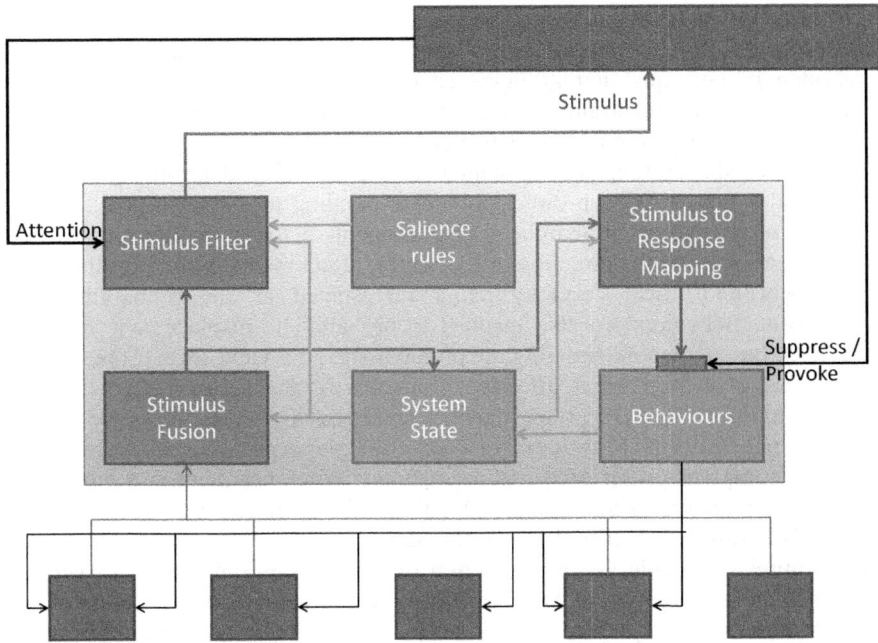

Fig. 3. The Generic controller model – showing connections to other generic controllers acting at higher and lower levels in the hierarchy

At the adaptive controller layer, each controller applies to relatively homogenous sub-systems where the local goals and behaviours are well understood, governance is supplied by ECA policies as well as predictive algorithms, responses are complex sub-system behaviors rather than simple atomic management actions. This corresponds to a typical autonomic system controller.

Our contribution is at the new, affective controller layer. This is a new type of controller that manages a "system of systems" across heterogeneous sub-systems with complex interrelationships. It uses the abstraction of emotional state with associated drives and behaviours to make decisions in situations too complex for deterministic rules or algorithms. Decision-making will be based on an attempt to maximise positive emotional goal-yield shifts in all situations. As shown in Fig. 2, (and in more detail in Fig. 3) the main method of passing information to upper layers is by way of stimuli messages, either as events or streams, where the upper layers assert what types of information they require by way of subscriptions (to represent attention or focus). The upper layer can then influence the lower layers by suppressing or provoking behavior selection as required.

This work is inspired by ongoing research in the cognitive science domain which speculates that higher order cognitive function (both processing and memory) is made possible by hierarchical abstraction of actions and concepts. Although there remains a debate about the physical validity of this approach (e.g. [17]) , it is clear that this hierarchical controller model is a well studied and validated approach for controlling and managing large, complex and distributed systems [18].

The affective controller is based upon a new approach to the closed-loop appraisal theory model [19] of emotion-based control. Stimuli are mapped to variables represented as concepts in ontologies enabling extensible open world reasoning. Affects are derived from stimuli through state machines which maintain episodic state and influence the attention of the controller and hence the stimuli that it receives. The core affect of the system is represented as a probability distribution in a multi-dimensional space, with each dimension corresponding to a system-goal. Appraised affects are represented as probabilistic displacement vectors in this space, with affect valence represented as the direction of the vector, affect intensity the magnitude of the displacement and affect certainty being represented as the probability of the displacement. Behaviors are also mapped to probabilistic displacement vectors and are selected based upon maximizing the probabilistic goal yield shift of the core affect [20]. In this way the current affective properties of the system acts as a bias or weighting to effect the perception, planning and behaviour selection processes of the affective controller. This system borrows affective aspects from control theory, semantics, computer vision, HCI and robotics and combines them in a novel way to produce an innovative system that is rich enough to be applied to regulating a system composed of complex, distributed, adaptive sub-systems.

In addition to its role as an abstraction of system state and behavior (including allowing limited prediction of future state) the emotional-behavioral model is at the top of the hierarchy of systems' control mechanisms, with current emotional state and drives influencing all other aspects of the system. It enables cross-activity goal analysis and prioritization leading to behavior or action selection through methods such as the yield shift theory of satisfaction [20]. Emotional state alters and parameterizes the perception sub-system, for example by changing the salience of stimuli, the degree of abstraction or stereotyping used in decision-making and the ontologies used for knowledge representation or stimuli categorization. In addition it influences local behaviors via parameterization and prioritization. Finally historical state is aggregated in the form of emotion memories [5] that abstract away from the details of specific stimuli, situations, behaviors and actions but which facilitate emotional recall and influence on future actions. The use of emotional state also enables cross-node communication of this abstract state, independent of system specifics, especially if there is an agreed emotional ontology [21] with, if necessary, agreed or negotiated semantics for specific objects of emotion.

Since the work described in this paper is still at an early stage a number of theoretical foundations need to be established. In the field of emotional processing it is recognized that there are four essential issues of an affective-behavioral model [12]:

- What features (e.g. intensity, valence, expectedness, certainty) of emotions should be represented in the models?
- How is an aggregate emotional state (core affect) aggregated from these emotional features?
- How do stimuli from the system and its sensed environment, when appraised against the (emotional and non-emotional) state and goals of the system, change these emotional features and the emotional state?
- How does the change of emotional state effect the cognitive and behavioral operation of the system, thus closing the inner and outer control loop?

A promising approach centers on the use of ontological semantics to represent the features required, to assist in the multi-layer abstraction and interoperability of the models and to drive the stimuli subscriptions between layers.

Since effective management of diversity is at the heart of our approach it will be necessary to iteratively validate the approach for a range of autonomic controller types, use cases and deployment domains. Thus it is proposed to build on the authors' expertise to examine existing autonomic communications systems [22] ranging from the backbone network, the access network to enterprise and home-area networks. The composite autonomic adaptions to be addressed via affective controls include: traffic analysis, routing, load balancing, service level assurance and threat monitoring. Although we have touched on a mechanism to implement and evaluate these design choices, further work is required to validate both these and alternative approaches.

3   Comparison to State of the Art

IBM's Autonomic Systems initiative has inspired a wealth of research that addresses infrastructure management complexity [1]. However it has largely focused on specialized, stove-piped, centralized autonomic management solutions. Even in such centralized systems, enabling effective human governance has proved problematic since, for example, a policy-based approach inevitably leads to a large rule-base that is both impenetrable to human intuition and specified at a granularity suited to the autonomic controls rather than the goals of the human administrator. In addition the domain (or adaptation) specific nature of many current autonomic systems makes it very hard to co-ordinate or optimize global behavior across multiple autonomic systems [3].

Affective approaches have surfaced before in the autonomics literature, especially in early work [11][12]. For example in [23] some limited affective processing is used to encapsulate abstract state for a specific adaptation domain however the key distinguishing features of our work are the concepts of using emotional state as an abstraction across a multitude of potentially competing adaptive controls, the application of appraisal theory control loops as a means to define generic behavioral models that can encapsulate the behavior of diverse adaptive systems and the use of affect (emotion) as a metaphor to simplify human governance of systems of adaptive systems.

Recent autonomics research has identified a need for a system of systems or a coordinated, federated approach for autonomic systems [3]. Unfortunately as system adaptability, scale and environmental dynamics increase it is no longer possible to design such systems based on relatively static, specific functional or business requirements. Instead more flexible systems are required that can adapt to new environmental factors, changing goals and stimuli. Fig. 4 illustrates the evolution that is envisaged with the new approach.

In order to illustrate the potential utility of the new approach, the next section provides some examples of how the new approach can be applied.

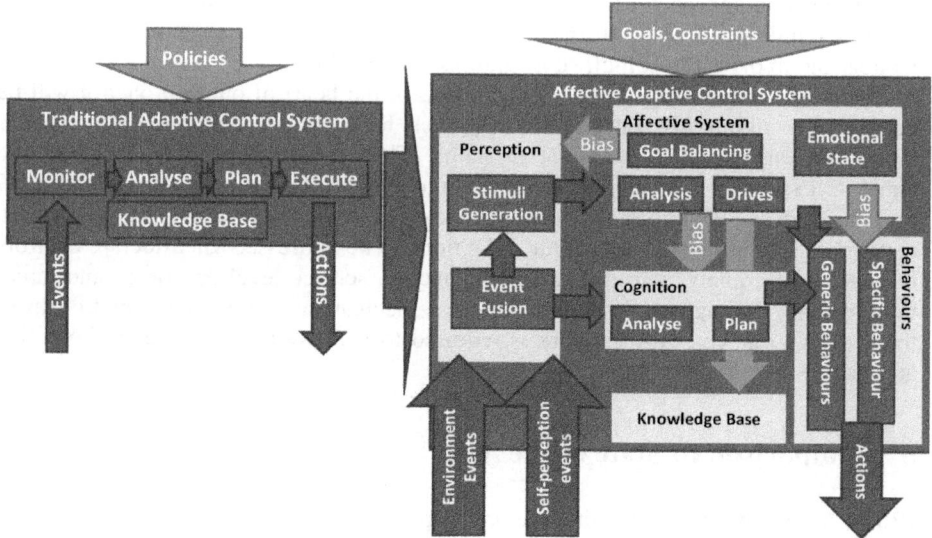

Fig. 4. Required evolution from the Autonomic to the Affective management approach

4 Application Examples

Existing autonomic systems already successfully demonstrate aspects of autonomic self management, however, as these systems scale, particularly in an autonomic communications domain, it becomes increasingly difficult for a single high-level governance stratum to adequately abstract and generalize about the health and optimality of the whole system. This is further exacerbated as heterogeneity increases.

Consider a very large system under attack from a low-intensity security attack (e.g. distributed Denial of Service attack). While individual adaptive parts of the system may try to recognize that an attack may be happening and may attempt to counteract the attack, a holistic approach is required to navigate the system to health. However, any automated governance system coordinating and overseeing the self-healing and self-protecting efforts of a large set of heterogeneous self-adaptive systems will be unable to provide different enforceable, concrete corrective measures to each of sub systems. The governance system can only adopt a high-level, abstract (concerned) stance, provide guidance or precedence to the self-adaptive sub-systems based on its holistic view, and request the sub-systems liaise with the governance system to coordinate the system to drive towards holistic health.

Consider also a system of system of self-managing network heterogeneous subnets. Each self managing subnet will have its own specialized but limited or local view of the state and optimality of the network as a whole. However, it is acknowledged that it is impractical to have a single oversight layer micro-manage the different constituent elements of the network, or even possess the low-level state and diverse expertise to do so. Any high-level automated governance system coordinating and overseeing the self management efforts for a large set of heterogeneous adaptive systems will be unable to provide detailed, enforceable, concrete corrective measures to each sub-system. It can only adopt a high-level, abstract stance, provide guidance or priorities based on its holistic view, and liaise with the sub-systems to coordinate and drive them towards holistic optimality.

Problems also arise where existing stovepipe autonomic network controllers need to be composed together or to be deployed on a different network technology. For example, standalone solutions for threat analysis, service level agreement (SLA) monitoring, network element load balancing and trust management, which must be effectively configured to work together to maximize network revenue, performance and safety. Experience shows that controlling and coordinating such systems traditionally requires extensive domain modeling, especially in terms of relatively rigid predictive behavioral models. Governance of such a system is deeply problematic since current event condition action (ECA) policies typically must be specified at a level that is too fine-grained to support human intuition about the high level business goals of such a system of adaptive systems. One solution is to build a replacement, multi-goal optimizing system (ignoring the real need to leverage existing investment) but the result is likely to be a more expensive and monolithic stovepiped autonomic system that must grudgingly co-habit with other adaptive systems. Another approach is to have a canonical, complete domain description, at multiple levels of abstraction, perhaps defined as a policy continuum, in an information model for the adaptive management system to draw upon and be driven by. However the rigidity of this approach, coupled with the need for comprehensive, timely, fine-grained and consistent models of the business, services and networks make it either expensive to deploy and maintain or likely to revert to the case of traditional incomplete domain models with no significant ability to adapt to dynamic service compositions or new behavior patterns for the system of systems.

5 Discussion

The goal of this work is to provide concrete breakthroughs in a number of fundamental research areas.

In the area of distributed intelligence and control, complex real-world ICT systems of adaptive systems have intelligence and control distributed throughout the system. Sub-systems may change their behavior in response to events (reactive control) or may have more dynamic, adaptive behavior within an autonomic controller. This work requires the use of affect models to represent, appraise and regulate the impact of composite, distributed, adaptive sub-system behaviors on overall system goals where individual sub-system behaviors are too complex to be traditionally modeled or reliably predicted.

Advances are also required in the fields of event processing, appraisal and filtering. ICT systems produce streams of messages about their state – events, errors, logs, alarms and so on. Processing this data to identify significant events that require behavioral changes quickly leads to data-overload. Hierarchical control systems typically address this problem by aggregating lower level events to provide 'summaries' to upper levels. However, to understand state changes that come from unexpected interactions between sub-systems, it is often necessary to analyze and correlate specific events from diverse sub-systems, hence higher level controllers must have access to lower level events in order to adapt correctly. The presented innovative architecture supports both bottom up, salience based messaging as well as a top-down attention model controlled by affective state to govern the flows of stimuli (events) between controllers in the hierarchy.

As adaptability, scale and the complexity of their environmental interactions increase it becomes impossible to design systems based on relatively static and specific functional or business requirements. The affective model presented in this paper will capture and operate on high-level system goals, providing a novel governance goal decomposition mechanism that is abstracted away from specific underlying technologies or controllers and can be extended to incorporate new high level goals or controllers as they become apparent.

The complexity of distributed IT systems is such that controllers rarely have a complete and reliable picture of the state of the systems that they control and it is generally difficult to understand events so that they can be reliably linked to changes in system state. It is planned to further design the affective appraisal model to deal with uncertainty and enable decision making even in situations where uncertainty is pervasive.

Many important issues in affective systems, neuroscience and psychology governing the use, modeling and effects of affect remain controversial. However, much criticism arises from the lack of definitive proof of the neurological or clinical accuracy of the approaches, not with the efficacy of these models when correctly applied in technological domains. Thus, the risk that advances in neuroscience or psychology could invalidate models, e.g. appraisal theory for humans, has little relevance to our application of them. Some affective systems research argues that placing emotions at the top of the control loop is insufficient and instead a more complex control architecture is required that is based on a synthesis between affect and other (cognitive) aspects of a system's controllers. However appraisal-based control has been demonstrated to be highly effective at decision-making in complex, real-time situations, e.g. human dialog maintenance, so it is likely that this concern is more relevant for building realistic artificial emotional-cognitive models rather than the applications considered here. A related observation is that emotional guidance is not always desirable in humans, even with cognitive mechanisms available to constrain the degree of emotion involved in making decisions. In this work, however, the affective controller will still be constrained by the goals and drives of the human overseer with additional engineering constraints operating at every level (reactive, adaptive, affective) of the control hierarchy. Finally, there are many pitfalls of affect-based HCI, but again they are not in scope for this work since the affect model is only envisaged here as a metaphor to simplify governance rather than to generate realistic synthetic emotions to promote human-machine empathy.

6   Conclusions

This paper proposes the basis of a systems theory for large-scale autonomic systems that supports integrated management without requiring standardisation on a single technology. In addition, if successful, the affective models deployed naturally lead to interdisciplinary research paths in cognitive and computer science in management system HCI, applications of emotional memory and the exploitation of social-emotional interactions for affective controller-based management systems.

The most significant novelty of this proposal is that it will develop an affective controller and build on the presented architecture in a way that can be applied to manage complex composed systems of heterogeneous adaptive systems where intelligence is distributed throughout the system and where federated sub-systems may adapt autonomously of their controllers according to their own local goals. The appraisal theory approach to stimulus processing and affect derivation, multi-dimensional core affect states, combined with standard hierarchical control models, is common in robotics and HCI. While the concept of mapping emotional states to a multi-dimensional core-affect space is not new, it has been primarily applied to problems of emotional expressions in virtual characters, or motivation inference of human operators, but the use of this approach to govern high-level decision making in complex, distributed multi-objective problem spaces is novel. In addition, the introduction of probability and uncertainty into this appraisal, the use of semantics to support extensibility of stimuli to variable derivation, and the use of episodic state machines as a means of exploring the effect of stimuli on system state and mapping particular emotional changes to particular causes is also entirely novel.

While there have been several previous (and somewhat successful) attempts at combining autonomic control with the emotional metaphor, these attempts have exclusively focused on centralized and monotonic systems, and always internal to the autonomic controller. A key novelty of this approach is to use the affective approach to govern multiple heterogeneous and distributed self-adapting systems, as a single holistic system, without breaking the operation of the underlying autonomous systems, rather to act as high-level holistic oversight.

Acknowledgement

This research is supported by the Science Foundation Ireland (Grant 08/SRC/I1403) (Federated, Autonomic End to End Communications Services Strategic Research Cluster (www.fame.ie)). The authors wish to thank Simon Dobson, Jose Lozano and Daniele Miorandi for valuable feedback during the preparation of this manuscript.

References

[1] Kephart, J.O., Chess, D.M.: The vision of autonomic computing. Computer 36(1), 41–50 (2003)
[2] Dobson, S., Denazis, S., Fernández, A., Gaïti, D., Gelenbe, E., Massacci, F., Nixon, P., Saffre, F., Schmidt, N., Zambonelli, F.: A survey of autonomic communications. ACM Transactions on Autonomous and Adaptive Systems 1(2), 223–259 (2006)
[3] Dobson, S., Sterritt, R., Nixon, P., Hinchey, M.: Fulfilling the vision of autonomic computing. IEEE Computer 43(1), 35–41 (2010)
[4] Clore, G.L., Palmer, J.: Affective guidance of intelligent agents: How emotion controls cognition. Cognitive Systems Research 10(1), 21–30 (2009)
[5] Velásquez, J.D.: When Robots Weep: Emotional Memories and Decision-Making. In: National Conference on Artificial Intelligence (AAAI 1998), Madison, Wi, USA (1998)

[6] Malfaz, M., Salichs, M.A.: A new architecture for autonomous robots based on emotions. In: Symposium on Intelligent Autonomous Vehicles, Lisbon, Portugal (July 2004)

[7] Velasquez, J.D.: A Computational Framework for Emotion-Based Control. In: Workshop on Grounding Emotions in Adaptive Systems, Conf. Simulat. Adapt. Behav. (1998)

[8] Murphy, R., Lisetti, C.L., Tardif, R., Irish, L., Gage, A.: Emotion-Based Control of Cooperating Heterogeneous Robots. IEEE Transactions on Robotics and Automation 18(5), 744–757 (2002)

[9] Tsankova, D.D.: Emotional Intervention on an Action Selection Mechanism Based on Artificial Immune Networks for Navigation of Autonomous Agents. Adaptive Behavior 17(2), 135–152 (2009)

[10] Bigus, J.P., Schlosnagle, D.A., Pilgrim, J.R., Mills, W.N., Diao, Y.: ABLE: A toolkit for building multiagent autonomic systems. IBM Systems Journal 41(3) (2002)

[11] Lee, A.: Emotional Attributes in Autonomic Computing Systems. In: Int'l Workshop on Database and Expert Systems Applications (DEXA 2003), Prague, Czech Republic (2003)

[12] Norman, D.A., Ortony, A., Russell, D.M.: Affect and Machine Design: Lessons for the Development of Autonomous Machines. IBM Systems Journal 42(1), 38–44 (2003)

[13] Bartneck, C., Lyons, M.J., Saerbeck, M.: The Relationship Between Emotion Models and Artificial Intelligence. In: Workshop on The Role of Emotion in Adaptive Behaviour And Cognitive Robotics, at the 10th International Conference on Simulation of Adaptive Behavior: From Animals to Animates (SAB 2008), Osaka (2008)

[14] Breazeal, C.: Function Meets Style: Insights From Emotion Theory Applied to HRI. IEEE Transactions in Systems, Man, and Cybernetics 34(2), 187–194 (2004)

[15] Michaud, F.: EMIB — Computational Architecture Based on Emotion and Motivation for Intentional Selection and Configuration of Behaviour-Producing Modules. Cognitive Science Quarterly (2002)

[16] Gratch, J., Marsella, S.: The Architectural Role of Emotion in Cognitive Systems. In: Gray, W.D. (ed.) Integrated Models of Cognitive Systems, pp. 230–242. Oxford University Press, New York (2007)

[17] Cohen, G.: Hierarchical models in cognition: Do they have psychological reality? European Journal of Cognitive Psychology 12(1), 1–36 (2000)

[18] Findeisen, W., Bailey, F.N., Brdys, M., Malinowski, K., Tatjewski, P., Wozniak, A.: Control and Coordination in Hierarchical Systems. John Wiley & Sons / I.I.A.S.A. (1980)

[19] Marsella, S., Gratch, J., Petta, P.: Computational Models of Emotion. In: Scherer, K.R., Bänziger, T., Roesch, E. (eds.) A Blueprint for an Affectively Competent Agent: Cross-Fertilization Between Emotion Psychology, Affective Neuroscience, and Affective Computing. Oxford University Press, Oxford (2010)

[20] Briggs, R.O., Reinig, B.A., de Vreede, G.J.: The yield shift theory of satisfaction and its application to the IS/IT domain. Journal of the Association for Information Systems 9(5), 267–293 (2008)

[21] López, J.M., Gil, R., García, R., Cearreta, I., Garay, N.: Towards an ontology for describing emotions. In: Lytras, M.D., Carroll, J.M., Damiani, E., Tennyson, R.D. (eds.) WSKS 2008. LNCS (LNAI), vol. 5288, pp. 96–104. Springer, Heidelberg (2008)

[22] Jennings, B., van der Meer, S., Balasubramaniam, S., Botvich, D., O'Foghlu, M., Donnelly, W., Strassner, J.: Towards Autonomic Management of Communications Networks. IEEE Commun. Mag. 45(10), 112–121 (2007)

[23] Sterritt, R.: Pulse monitoring: extending the health-check for the autonomic grid. In: IEEE Int'l Conference on Industrial Informatics (INDIN 2003), August 21-24, pp. 433–440 (2003)

A Policy Authoring Process and DEN-ng Model Extension for Federation Governance

Jason Barron[1], Steven Davy[1], Brendan Jennings[1], and John Strassner[2]

[1] FAME, Telecommunications Software & Systems Group,
Waterford Institute of Technology, Ireland
{jbarron,sdavy,bjennings}@tssg.org
[2] IT Convergence Engineering Division,
Pohang University of Science and Technology (POSTECH), Korea
johns@postech.ac.kr

Abstract. To support rapidly evolving business models, communications network management systems are increasingly being *federated* to provide more flexible, end-to-end service management. In the future, such federation will need to be achieved dynamically, thus management systems will need to incorporate capabilities supporting negotiation of federations and management of their lifecycle. We discuss how federations can be governed via negotiated *federation-level policies*, that should be consistent with the relevant *local policies* of individual federation members. We describe a policy authoring process, outlining the steps to be taken when local or federation-level policies are created, modified or withdrawn. As this process depends on the presence of a rich system model for policy analysis we describe an extension to DEN-ng that models governance of federated domains. Finally, we outline a case study relating to inter-organisation XMPP federations to illustrate the policy authoring process.

1 Introduction

Current network domains are predominantly managed on an individual basis, the aim being to optimise the transfer of information within administrative boundaries. Coordination across domain boundaries does exist, however its scope is limited primarily to participation in end-to-end routing protocols, network peering arrangements and exchange of certain management information (in particular for charging and billing purposes). Furthermore, such coordination is static in nature, with changes requiring time consuming negotiations and coordinated deployment by network operators. However, due to deregulation and conssequent increases in marketplace competition there is a strong impetus for network operators to support more flexible business models—a good example is that of virtual operators owning little or no infrastructure of their own, so that service delivery is always based on crossing multiple administrative domains. To this end we argue that network management systems need to be evolved to support *federations*, which we view as persistant agreements between organisations,

R. Brennan, J. Fleck II, and S. van der Meer (Eds.): MACE 2010, LNCS 6473, pp. 73–86, 2010.

parts or organisations and/or individuals that enable them share information or capabilities in a controlled manner.

To provide for creation and management of federations of communications networks their management systems will need to cooperate closely. This cooperation will encompasses the exhange of monitoring and configuration data and possibly the delegation of authority to other federation members to manage their resources. We believe that this form of cooperation is most readily achieveable where management systems apply Policy-based Management (PBM) paradigm. In previous work [5] we addressed the concept of a *Policy Continuum,* in which policies at different levels of abstraction are linked in order to allow high level goals expressed using business concepts (e.g. customer, service) to be translated into appropriate low-level device configurations (e.g. CLI-based configuration of router traffic shaping and queuing). Implementation of the policy continuum enables these constituencies, who understand different concepts and use different terminologies, to manipulate sets of policy representations at a view appropriate to them, and to have those view-specific representations mapped to equivalent representations at views appropriate for manipulation by other constituencies.

If we assume that members of a federation each realise a policy continuum to manage their local resources then we can envisage sets of "federation-level" policies that relate to their participation in a given federation. For the federation as a whole, governance will be provided by the collection of federation-level policies from each federation member, so these policies must be negotiated by the federation members in line with federation goals. Furthermore, each federation member will need to ensure that its local policies are consistent with the federation-level policies of each of the federations it is a member of. Maintaining this consistency is a complex task since changes to federation-level policies may have implications for local policies and vice versa. In this paper we outline an extension of the policy authoring process described in [5] that outlines the policy analysis steps that need to be taken to ensure consistency between local and federation-level policies when policies are created, modified or deleted. Since policy analysis requires detailed system models we also describe an extension to the DEN-ng information model that facilitates modelling of federation domains and the policies that govern them; this is a useful first step towards using DEN-ng for analysis of consistency between local and federation-level policies.

The paper is structured as follows: §2 outlines related work on policy management of federations; §3 outlines the policy authoring process; whilst §4 describes the DEN-ng federated domain model. In §5 we discuss a case study for application of the policy authoring process in the context of the creation of an eXtensible Messaging and Presence Protocol (XMPP) federation between two enterprises. Finally, §6 summaries the paper and outlines areas for further investigation.

2   Related Work

The majority of the published literature concerning network management concentrates on aspects of maximising the performance of network domains controlled by a single organisation. However in the broader literature on computing systems cooperation between autonomous systems has been addressed. An early example is the work of Heimbigner and McLeod [7], who define an federation architecture and protocol for heterogeneous, autonomous databases, in which a central authority coordinates exchange of data and transactions. A federal dictionary is used to store the topology of the federation and is responsible for adding new components to the federation. This work is restricted to only working with federated databases and is heavily dependent on a single central authority for federation management. More recently, Machiraju et al. [10] present an architecture, object model, components and protocols for a management overlay for federated web service management. In this management overlay proxies for the web services coordinate to manage that service level agreements are adhered to. However, it does not address interaction of the management overlays with the management systems of the hosting environments for individual web services.

In the policy-based management literature Hull et al. [8] describe a framework to support federated policy management with in a single administrative domain—they consider "federations" of multiple policy engines and argue that network administrators should be able to deploy a single policy rule set and have appropriate rules deployed on each policy engine in the federation. This view of federation does not correspond to ours; it is closer in conception to the policy continuum in which policies specified at a high level of abstraction can be refined for deployment on groups of policy engines. Bhatti et al. [2] describe X-FEDERATE, a framework for access control management within federations. Their approach is to specify an XML-based policy specification language and an enforcement architecture that constitutes an extension of the well-known Role-Based Access Control (RBAC) model. Their work concentrates on security management aspects and again does not consider the issue of maintaining consistency between federation-level and local policies.

Feeney et al. [6] propose an approach to managing communities (for example open source software project developer communities) using policy based management. They argue that such communities typcially impose a management hierarchy which can be readily modelled in a policy management system. Subcommunities in a hierarchy can be delegated authority over a specified set of resources or services and within these constraints can specify and enforce their own "local" policies. When policies are created or modified they can be checked for conflicts with other local policies and, if no conflicts exist, can be passed to the parent community where potential conflicts can again be identified. Parent policies are given precedence in case of conflicts, thus the policy hierarchy provides a well defined means of conflict resolution. This work is close in spirit to our work since it provides a means for ensuring consistency between policies in a policy hierarchy. Indeed extensions of community-based management approach [3,9] address management of federations directly, introducing the concept of a *Federal Relationship Manager (FRM)* component, associated with individual federation members, that controls the delegation of capabilities to other federation members.

As discussed in the introduction this paper extends the (single domain) policy authoring process we specified in [4,5]. This process enables experts responsible for authoring policies at different levels of a policy continuum identify if their new or modified policies potentially conflict with currently deployed policies, at that level or at other levels of the policy continuum. The process comprises the following steps. If a policy is created, modified at a given policy continuum level the process initially ascertains if the "candidate" policy still fulfills its role of being one of a group of policies at that level which form a valid refinement of one or more policies at the next level up in the contiuum. If this is the case the process checks whether the policy conflicts with any other policies at the same continuum level. Finally the policy is refined into one or more policies in the next level down in the hierarchy and a conflict check is made at that level. This refinement/conflict analysis is iterated until a set of deployable policies (typcially device configuration commands) are generated. If, at any stage a potential conflict is identified the policy author(s) at that level of the policy continuum are notified and are responsible if the warning should be ignored or if the conflict should be resoved. All of the anaylsis steps assume the presence of a rich system model used by the various policy analysis processes (policy refinement, policy refinement validation and policy conflct analysis). For our previous work we have used the DEN-ng information model, which includes a rich policy model and the ability to associate modelled policies to a management domain [12].

3   Policy Authoring Process with Federation Support

As outlined above our previous work on policy authoring and analysis was concerned only within maintaining consistency between policy representations with a single policy continuum used to govern a single network domain. When a network is part of a federation we have these "local" policies, but also as "federation-level" policies, so that, as depicted in Figure 1, sub-groups of the former embody the management logic required to realise the latter. Federation-level policies associated with one network operation are linked with other policies in other federation members, thereby enforcing the federation agreement in place between the participants. For example, a federation agreement may allow a network operator configure a set-top box in a customer's home area network; thus the home area network management system will have a federation-level policy allowing the network operator configure aspects of the set-top box, whilst the network operator may have policies controlling when such configurations are applied.

Whilst Figure 1 shows a federation involving two members it should be noted that many federations will have many members (possibly with members continuously joining and leaving) and that individual members may be involved in many federations. Given this, a network operator will be faced with the challenge of managing its resources in a manner that meets its own local business goals, whilst also meeting its commitments to participation in one or more federations. In a dynamic environment we can expect the changes in local or federation-level policies will be relatively frequent; each such change may require the network

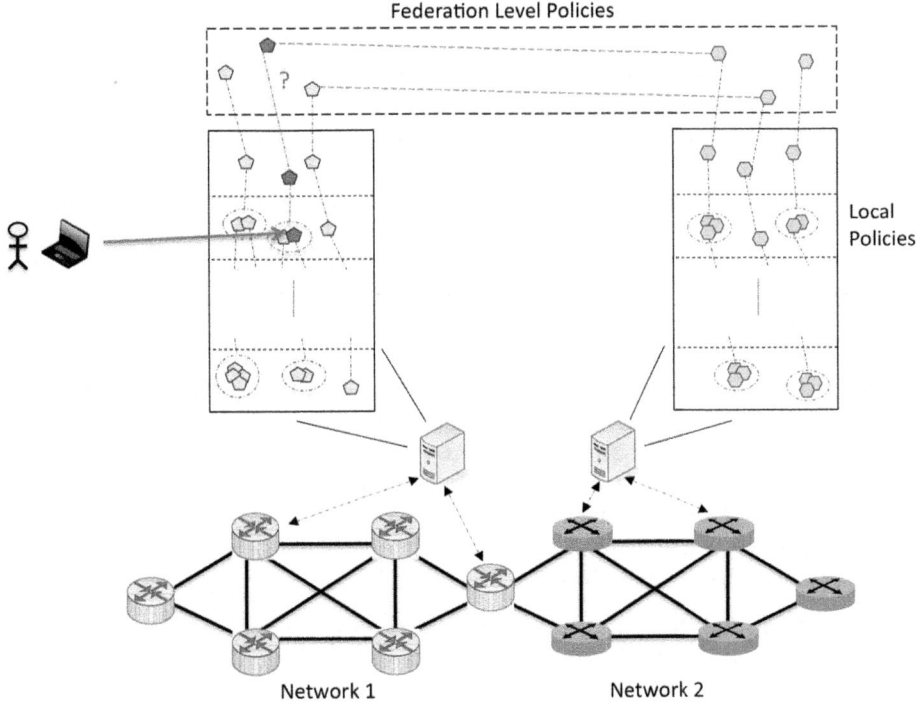

Fig. 1. Local and Federation-level Policies

operator to re-assess whether its deployed policies are *consistent* and whether they achieve the best possible result given availabe resources and demand levels. Our goal is to develop a policy authoring process and associated analysis tools that will help automate this assessment process.

We identify the following cases in which policy changes will require assesment of the consistency between local and federation-level policies:

1. *Local Policy or Policies Created, Modified or Deleted*

   At some level of the local policy continuum a policy author attempts to change one or more of the deployed policies. According to our single domain authoring process [5], the changes are analysed to ascertain if the modified policies are still valid refinements of the linked policies in the next level up the continuum. If this is not the case the policy author at that upper level is notified. If that author decrees that a change can be made at its level then the process is iterated until the top level of the continuum is reached. In the enhanced process the proposed change in local policies will (as illustrated in Figure 1) be assessed in terms of its impact on the relevant federation-level policies in each of the federations these local policies are associated with. If the proposed changes mean that the federation level policies are invalidated there are two options: either the proposed change is rejected, or the relevant federation agreements (and federation-level policies) are re-negotiated;

2. *Renegotiation of Federation-level Policies*

   As well as local policy changes triggering renegotiation of federation agreements and federation-level policies the network operator may itself trigger the re-negotiation. Assuming that federation negotiation is carried out by some multi-step process of bid and counter-bid, then at each step a proposed set of federation-level policies will need to be assessed. Part of this assessement is likely to involve testing whether a combination of already deployed local policies and new policies can effect the behaviour embodied in the federation-level policies. If this is possible, then the impact of introducing new local policies—in terms of the possibility of them introducing conflicts as they are refined down through the policy continuum and in terms of any impact they may have on the ability to meet commitments to other federations—will need to be analysed. The federation-level policies resulting from a negotiation process would be expected to be consistent with pre-existing local policies and the operator's participation in other federations;

3. *Another Member Triggers Re-negotiation of Federation Policies*

   As well as a federation member wishing to change its own local or federation-level policies other federation members can trigger renegotiations, in which case the steps outlined in point 2 will again be required.

It should be noted that this policy authoring process independent of the manner in which federations themselves are governed. As described in §4 federations may be controlled by a single central manager or being collectively governed by peer managers. Our authoring process addresses only the interactions between local and federation-level policies, it does not make any assumptions regarding how the federation-level policies are negotiated. Algorithm 1 outlines the steps to be taken in the authoring process when a prpoosed modification is made to an operator's policies. Some of these steps can be automated via policy analysis process that use system models to assess relationships between polcies, whilst others require decisions from (human) policy authors responsible for policies relating to different policy continuum levels and federations.

4   DEN-ng Federated Domain Model

The DEN-ng as outlined by Strassner [11] is an object-oriented information model that can be used to represent the business and system entities of a network. DEN-ng representations are independent of any specific type of repository, software usage, or access protocol which makes DEN-ng suitable for describing how different management information is related to each other and because the business and system entities are represented in generic form in the information model; they can be translated quite easily to platform-specific implementations. The DEN-ng domain model as illustrated in Figure 2 addresses the representation of management domains; where a domain is defined as a group of entities (resources, services, devices, etc.) that share a common goal. They can be organised hierarchically or linearly and are uniquely addressable within their respective domains. A management domain adds three important behavioural

Algorithm 1. Modify a policy considering federation agreements.

ModifyPolicy : $(PolicyRule \times PolicyRule \times PolicyContinuum \times \mathbb{P}Federation) \to \mathbf{B}$

ModifyPolicyContinuum $(p_{old}, p_{new}, pc, fs) \triangleq$

if $p_{old} \in$ **GetFederationPolicies** (fs)

then

$\forall ag_f \in$ **AnalyseFederationAgreements** (p_{new}, pc, fs)
  if $failed \mid rejected \to$ **ReNegotiateAgreement** (p_{old}, ag_f)
  then
      NotifyFederationPolicyAuthor $(p_{old}, ag_f) \to return$ **false**
  else
    $\forall p_{pc1} =$ **RefinePolicyToLevel$_1$** (p_{new}, pc) :
      if $conflict \to$ **AnalyseForPolicyConflict** (p_{pc1}, pc)
      then
          NotifyPolicyContinuumLevelAuthor$_1$ $(p_{new}, p_{pc1}) \to return$ **false**
      else
      if $invalidated \to$ **ValidateFederationAgreements** (p_{pc1}, fs)
      then
          ReNegotiateAgreements (p_{pc1}, fs)

else if $p_{old} \in$ **GetLevelPolicies$_1$** (pc)

then

    if $invalidated \to$ **ValidateFederationAgreements** (p_{new}, fs)

    then

        ReNegotiateAgreements (p_{new}, fs)

else$-$ *Continue with original authoring process*

$\forall p_{parent} \in$ **GetPolicyParents** $(p_{old}) pc$:

  if *not* **VerifyPolicyContinuum** $(p_{parent}, p_{new}, pc)$
  then
      NotifyCurrentAuthor (p_{parent})
      return **false**

if $\mathbb{P}\mathbf{p_{cnf}} =$ **AnalysePolicyConflict** (p_{new}, pc)

then

  $\forall p_{cnf} \in$ **PotentialConflictList** $(p_{new}) pc$:
    $\forall p_{parcnf} \in$ **GetPolicyParents** $(p_{cnf}) pc$:
        NotifyCurrentAuthor (p_{parcnf})
    NotifyCurrentAuthor (p_{cnf})
    return **false**

else

  $\forall p_{oldcld} \in$ **GetPolicyChildren** (p_{old}, pc) :
      DeletePolicy (p_{oldcld}, pc)
  $\forall p_{ref} =$ **RefinePolicy** (p_{new}, pc) :
      AddPolicy $\left(\pi^1 \circ pc\left(p_{new}\right), p_{ref}\right) pc$
  VerifyPolicyContinuum (p_{new}, p_{ref}, pc)

CommitChange (p_{old}, p_{new}, pc)

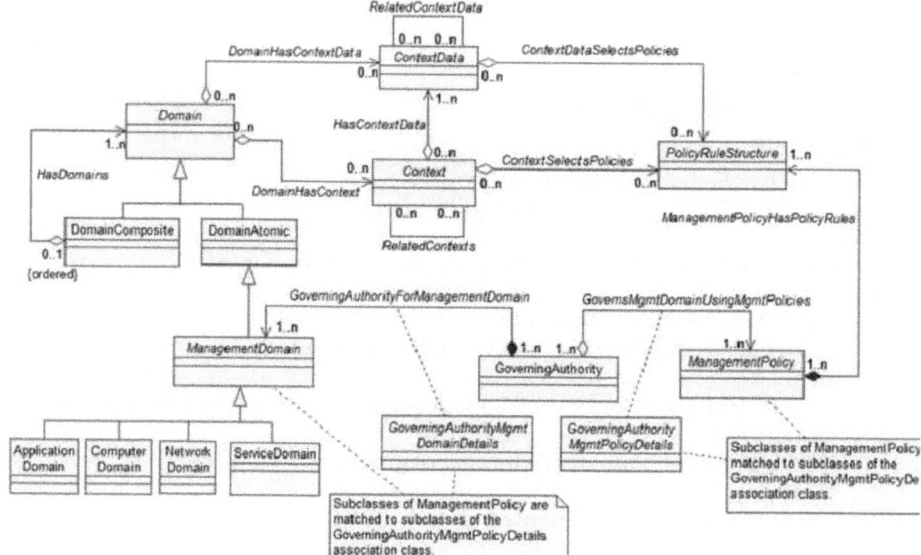

Fig. 2. Original DEN-ng Domain Model

features to a domain: (a) it defines a common set of administrators (user, group of users, and/or organisation(s)) to control its entities, (b) it defines a set of applications for various administration tasks (monitoring, configuration, etc.), (c) it defines a common set of management mechanisms, such as policy rules, that are used by the administration tasks. A domain has context data (i.e. time of day, environment settings, etc.) that can be used when specifying policy rules.

The DEN-ng domain model has been extended to include support for federated domains as illustrated in Figure 3. Context data can be obtained from each service provder domain to give an overall view of context data for a federation of service providers. This type of data can be used to assist in specifying federation-level policies and for policy conflict analysis processes. This DEN-ng extension defines four types of federated domains which are characterised according to the federation's governance structure and continuum of governance mechanisms. The continuum is constrained by autonomy on the one side and local and/or global rules which must be adhered to on the other side. This leads to a range of possible governance structures with the most fundamental ones being:

1. A single central authority that governs all other federation participants through the use of policy (i.e., single central authority, subservient domains, only global policy rules).
2. A single central authority that organises the actions of the other federation participants (i.e., single central authority, autonomous domains, local and global policy rules).

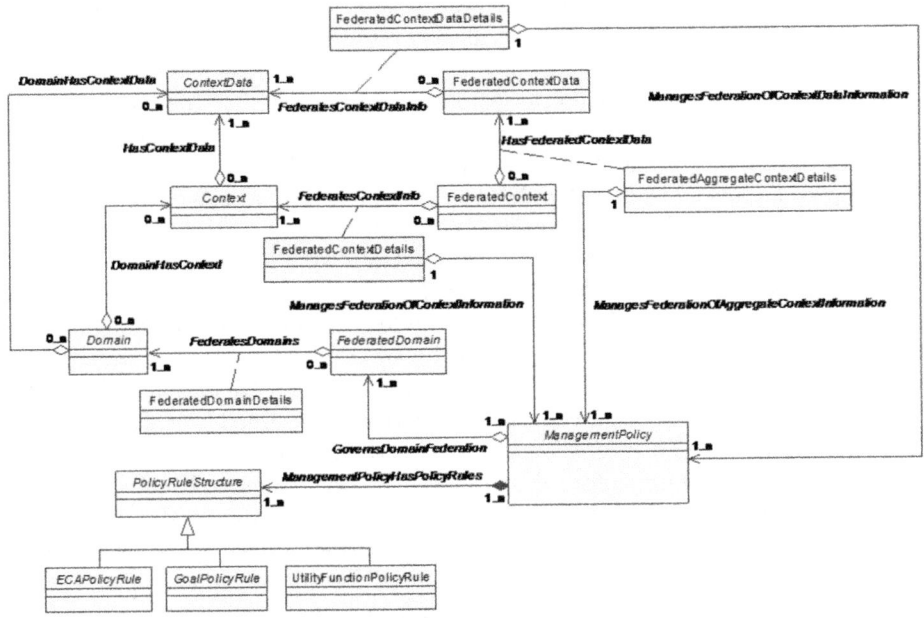

Fig. 3. New DEN-ng Federated Domain Model

3. A distributed set of authorities that use agreed-upon mechanisms of governance to specify rules that each federation participant must abide by while remaining somewhat autonomous (i.e., distributed authority, autonomous domains, local and global policy rules).
4. A distributed set of authorities that dictate policy to be adhered to by subservient federation participants (i.e., distributed authority, subservient domains, global policy rules only).

5 Case Study

We now describe an application of the DEN-ng federated domain model and federated authoring process based on a XMPP communication test-bed scenario. The scenario is based on two enterprises, AAA Consultancy, a software consultancy company that has been contracted to provide consultancy services to IS Bank, a financial institution. Both enterprises have a hierarchical XMPP grouping structure based on their internal organisational hierarchy. A member of the Java consultants group from the consultancy company has been contracted to provide consultancy services and as such will be stationed at the bank's premise for the majority of the contract. While stationed at the bank, the Java consultant will be a temporary member of the software development group (SD) and will require participation in XMPP communication services such as Instant Messaging (IM), multi-party chat and document transfer with the group leader of that particular SD group within the bank, the Chief Technology Officer (CTO) of the bank. The Java consultant will also require XMPP communication services with its in-house Java consultants group back in the consultancy company while stationed at the bank. Furthermore, while stationed at the bank, the Java consultant will not be permitted to participate in any XMPP communication services available with any other members of the SD group of which he is a temporary member or any other XMPP groups or individuals within the bank.

This will require both enterprises to federate their XMPP communication services. In order to control the federation of the XMPP communication services, a high-level federation policy can be specified. This federation policy can specify the structure and required behaviour of the federation, so as to manage XMPP communications traffic flowing between the two domains. A negotiation process will be required between the two domains in order to create and agree upon this federation-level policy. This negotiation process is assumed to exist and is not part of this work. The federation policy can then be translated into a system-level policy before being enforced on devices. In this scenario, XACML has been chosen for the system-level policy.

The application process is based on previous work outlined by Barrett et al. [1] and involves the the creation of the required federation Domain Specific Language (DSL). An information model contains extraneous information that is not required to produce a federation DSL. As a result only the required information is tagged and extracted from the DEN-ng federated model for the purposes of generation of the federation DSL and accompanying tools. A DSL generated from the DEN-ng federated domain model can be used to construct an object model of the federated domains. This federation DSL includes an accompanying parser and editor that are aware of the types of entities that can be linked to one another and in exactly what manner, as this information has been previously specified in the information model. This has the added bonus of preventing the user from describing configurations of the federated domains that are inconsistent with the information model. A federation DSL can be used to represent not only the entities that exist within federated domains, but also the interactions that are permitted between those entities.

Following on from the federation DSL creation process, a federation-level policy can be specified. Each federation participant can make use of the federated policy authoring process to aid in the specification of the federation-level policy as this process can check if the newly created or modified policy will conflict with previously deployed local/federation policies. Once the federation-level policy has been checked for any possible conflicts, each federation participant can then translate the federation policy into system-level policies suited to the policy system running within their own domains. An example of one such federation-level policy specified from a federation DSL is depicted in Figure 4. This policy specifies the structure and behaviour of the AAA Consultancy and IS Bank federated domains and the constraints under which this federation is allowed to operate. In order for XMPP communication to take place between these federated domains, a single federation policy that maps to four system-level (XACML) policies will

```
Document {
//Governing Authorities and Federations
GoverningAuthority ("entA") {
 Domain ("AAAConsultancy") {
   Entities { Entity("JavaConsultant") Entity("JavaConsultancy") Entity("EntACTO") Entity("Sales")}
   Contexts { Context("JavaConsultancy") ("notShared")}
   Policies { ("polset1") }
    }//end Domain
    }//end GoverningAuthority

GoverningAuthority ("entB") {
 Domain ("ISBank") {
   Entities { Entity("Contractors") Entity("SoftwareDevelopment") Entity("EntBCTO") Entity("GroupLeader")}
   Contexts { Context("Contractors") ("notShared")}
   Policies { ("polset2")}
  }//end Domain
 }//end GoverningAuthority

Federation ("fedAB") {
//Contract of the federation is the context
    Domains { ("entA") ("entB") }
    Context { ("JavaConsultant from entA isContracted to entB")
                //few sentences regarding the terms of the contract
                ("Contractors isShared")}
    FedPolicies { ("fedPolicy")}
            }//end Federation

//Local and Federation Policies

PolicyRep ("polset1") { Subject ("JavaConsultant") Action("canMessage") Resource("JavaConsultancy");
                        Subject ("JavaConsultancy") Action("canMessage") Resource("JavaConsultant");
                        Subject ("JavaConsultant") Action("canMessage") Resource("EntACTO");
                        Subject ("EntACTO") Action("canMessage") Resource("JavaConsultant");
                        Subject ("JavaConsultancy") Action("canMessage") Resource("EntACTO");
                        Subject ("EntACTO") Action("canMessage") Resource("JavaConsultancy");
                        Subject ("Sales") Action("canMessage") Resource("EntACTO");
                        Subject ("EntACTO") Action("canMessage") Resource("Sales");
                        }//end PolicyRep

PolicyRep ("polset2") { Subject ("Contractors") Action("canMessage") Resource("EntBCTO");
                        Subject ("EntBCTO") Action("canMessage") Resource("Contractors");
                        Subject ("Contractors") Action("canMessage") Resource("GroupLeader");
                        Subject ("GroupLeader") Action("canMessage") Resource("Contractors");
                        Subject ("SoftwareDevelopment") Action("canMessage") Resource("EntBCTO");
                        Subject ("EntBCTO") Action("canMessage") Resource("SoftwareDevelopment");
                        }//end PolicyRep

FedPolicyRep ("fedPolicy") Context ("fedAB") {
                        Subject ("JavaConsultant") Action("canMessage") Resource("JavaConsultancy");
                        Subject ("JavaConsultancy") Action("canMessage") Resource("JavaConsultant");
                        Subject ("Sales") Action("canMessage") Resource("EntBCTO");
                        Subject ("EntBCTO") Action("canMessage") Resource("Sales");
                        }//endFedPolicyRep

}//end Document
```

Fig. 4. Federation Policy

need to be specified and deployed (two policies per federation participant); one policy to allow outgoing XMPP traffic and one policy to allow incoming XMPP traffic in each domain.

The federated XMPP architecture depicted in Figure 5 is in place within the two domains and consists of an open-source XMPP server, an Intercepter and a XACML policy server. Openfire[1] is an open-source XMPP server, written in Java. It supports various XMPP communications services such as IM, group

---

[1] Openfire, [Online] Available:
   http://www.igniterealtime.org/projects/openfire/

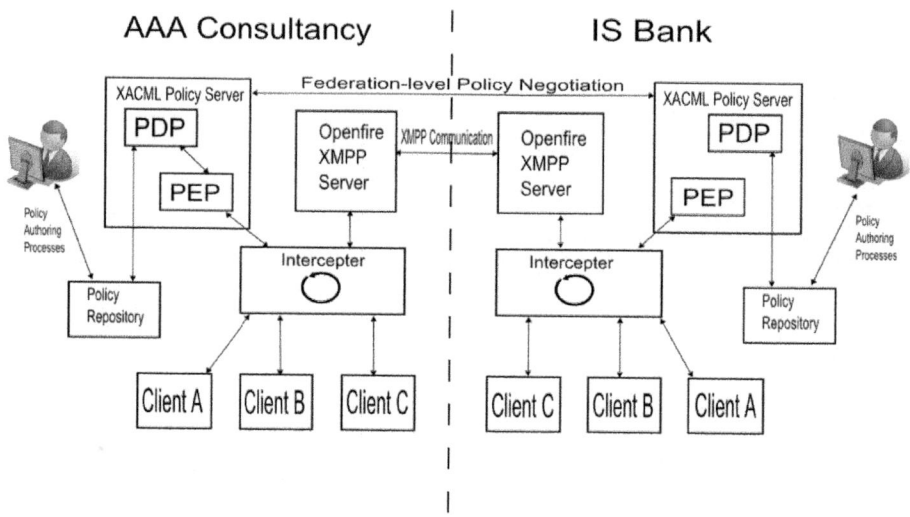

Fig. 5. Federated XMPP Architecture

chat, file transfer, etc., and uses the XMPP protocol for real time communication. XMPP is designed using a federated, client-server architecture. Server federation is a common means of spreading resource usage and control between Internet services. In a federated architecture, each server is responsible for controlling all activities within its own domain and works cooperatively with servers in other domains as equal peers. In XMPP, each client connects to the server that controls its XMPP domain. This server is responsible for authentication, message delivery and maintaining presence information for all users within the domain. An intercepter was implemented in Java to intercept XMPP packets travelling between the XMPP client and server with the aim of applying policy rules to the type of communication being sought. The Intercepter is basically a modified XMPP server that can intercept all XMPP packets travelling through it or individual types of XMPP packets such as Info/Query (IQ) packets, message packets or presence packets. The main tasks of the Intercepter are to forward XMPP packets to the XACML policy server, specifically the Policy Enforcement Point (PEP) component of the XACML policy server, process the response to the policy decision received from the PEP by either routing the XMPP packet to the XMPP server for delivery if the policy rule permits or returning an information message back to the XMPP client advising that the type of XMPP communication service being sought was denied.

Sun's XACML[2], is an open-source implementation of the OASIS XACML standard, written in the Java programming language. It consists of a set of Java classes that understand the XACML language, as well as the rules about how

---

[2] S. Proctor, Sun's XACML Implementation, [Online] Available(23/8/2010): `http://sunxacml.sourceforge.net/`

to process requests and how to manage attributes and other related data. The XACML policy server consists of two main components, a PEP for creating policy requests and a Policy Decision Point (PDP) for loading policies and making policy decisions. The PDP loads policies from a policy repository and makes decisions based on loaded policies and requests forwarded to it from the PEP. The policy repository can be a database or an Lightweight Directory Access Protocol (LDAP) system.

6   Conclusions

Market pressures are pushing network operators toward greater federation of their networks with each other and with their customers' networks. Whilst in the past such federations were limited in scope, statically define and long lasting the current trend is towards a much more dynamic environment in which federations will be formed for different purposes, will be much more numerous and may be relatively short lived and have changing membership profiles. To support this network operators require flexible tools to help them manage their networks in a manner cognisant of their commitments to federations in which they participate.

As an initial step toward developing such tools we have introduced an outline policy authoring process whose steps ensure that local policies are kept consistent with federation-level policies as individual policies are created, modified or withdrawn. We also describe an extension to DEN-ng to facilitate modelling of federated domains. Future work will concentrate on the investigation of techniques to automatically assess, based on knowledge embodied in system models, the likely impact of changes to local policies on federation-level policies and vice versa.

Acknowledgement

This work has been funded by the Science Foundation Ireland via the FAME strategic research cluster (http://www.fame.ie), grant no. 08/SRC/I1403.

References

1. Barrett, K., Davy, S., Strassner, J., Jennings, B., van der Meer, S., Donnelly, W.: A Model based Approach for Policy Tool Generation and Policy Analysis. In: Proc. 2007 IEEE Global Information Infrastructure Symposium (GIIS 2007), pp. 99–105 (2007)
2. Bhatti, R., Bertino, E., Ghafoor, A.: X-FEDERATE: A Policy Engineering Framework for Federated Access Management. IEEE Transactions on Software Engineering 32, 330–346 (2006)
3. Brennan, R., Lewis, D., Keeney, J., Etzioni, Z., Feeney, K., O' Sullivan, D., Lozano, J.A., Jennings, B.: Policy-based Integration of Multi-provider Digital Home Services. IEEE Network 23(6), 50–56 (2009)

4. Davy, S., Jennings, B., Strassner, J.: The Policy Continuum – A Formal Model. In: Proc. 2nd IEEE International Workshop on Modelling Autonomic Communications Environments (MACE 2007), pp. 65–79 (2007)
5. Davy, S., Jennings, B., Strassner, J.: The Policy Continuum – Policy Authoring and Conflict Analysis. Computer Communications 31, 2981–2995 (2008)
6. Feeney, K., Lewis, D., Wade, V.: Policy based Management for Internet Communities. In: Proc. 5th IEEE International Workshop on Policies for Distributed Systems and Networks (POLICY 2004), pp. 23–32 (2004)
7. Heimbigner, D., McLeod, D.: A Federated Architecture for Information Management. ACM Transactions on Information Systems 3(3), 278 (1985)
8. Hull, R., Kumar, B., Lieuwen, D.: Towards Federated Policy Management. In: Proc. 4th IEEE International Workshop on Policies for Distributed Systems and Networks (POLICY 2003), pp. 183–194 (2003)
9. Jennings, B., Feeney, K., Brennan, R., Balasubramaniam, S., Botvich, D., van der Meer, S.: Federating Autonomic Network Management Systems for Flexible Control of End-to-end Communications Services. In: Autonomic Network Management Principles. Elsevier, Amsterdam (2010s) (to appear)
10. Machiraju, V., Sahai, A., Van Moorsel, A.: Web Services Management Network: An Overlay Network for Federated Service Management. In: Proc. 8th IFIP/IEEE International Symposium on Integrated Network Management (IM 2003), vol. 3, pp. 351–364 (2003)
11. Strassner, J.: DEN-ng: Achieving Business-driven Network Management. In: Proc. 2002 IEEE/IFIP Network Operations and Management Symposium (NOMS 2002), pp. 753–766 (2002)
12. Strassner, J.: Policy-Based Network Management: Solutions for the Next Generation. The Morgan Kaufmann Series in Networking. Morgan Kaufmann, San Francisco (2003)
13. Strassner, J., de Souza, J., van der Meer, S., Davy, S., Barrett, K., Raymer, D., Samudrala, S.: The Design of a New Policy Model to Support Ontology-Driven Reasoning for Autonomic Networking. Journal of Network and Systems Management 17, 5–32 (2009)

An Introduction to Network Stack Design Using Software Design Patterns

Patrick Phelan, Zohra Boudjemil, Miguel Ponce de Leon, and Sven van der Meer

Waterford Institute of Technology
Telecommunications Software & Systems Group
Cork Road, Waterford, Ireland
{pphelan,zboudjemil,miguelpdl,vdmeer}@tssg.org

Abstract. "Tenet 1: Let 1000 networks bloom". This is the first principle of the EU IST project 4WARD and sets out one of the primary goals of this project – to explore new approaches that will allow present and future networks to be interoperable within a common architectural framework. As part of our work, we propose a software architecture for the future Internet realizing this core goal. This paper presents a conceptual introduction to our proposed architecture, which embraces simplicity and minimalism. Our architectural framework proposes a component-based architecture consisting of building blocks of reusable functionality, components that allow the construction of these building blocks and the composition of complex functionality, control elements facilitating communication between blocks, and a repository of building blocks. The architecture allows for rapid composition of federations of components, enabling an easy transition from present network infrastructure towards the future Internet and realizing the on-demand creation and configuration of protocol stacks for components.

1   Introduction

The concept of layering evolved in the late 1960s and 1970s in the design of operating systems and software in general. Layering is an expansion of the "black box" concept developed by Norbert Weiner. In communications, the idea of layering was standardized in the Reference Model for Open Systems Interconnection, commonly known as the OSI 7-layer model. Today, layered architectures form one of the most fundamental structures of network design today. They adopt a modularized and often distributed approach to network coordination. Each layer controls a subset of decision parameters and variables from other layers; in a protocol stack, this hides the complexity of the layer below and provides a service to the layer above. The design pattern of layering is widely recognized as one of the key reasons for the success of data networks and the Internet [15].

However, layering in the network stack seems to be having difficulties in adjusting to new protocols and services, as evidenced by the large and ever growing interest in cross-layer design over the last few years. Is this a problem with the current implementation of layering within the network stack, or a problem with the layering

R. Brennan, J. Fleck II, and S. van der Meer (Eds.): MACE 2010, LNCS 6473, pp. 87–99, 2010.

design pattern? When a cross layer approach is broken down, it is simply a new ordering of the network stack – in other words, layering is still present within the network stack, which is simply re-ordered.

Is the real problem a very simple one: the network stack as we know it is simply too rigidly implemented? Certainly, protocols such as ATM and MPLS cannot be strictly classified as "layer n", as they embody principles from multiple layers. This is an example of how individual layers are designed to be too aware and dependent on their neighboring layers. This implicit knowledge and interlinking was primarily the result of performance optimizations in the early days of networks, which blurred boundaries between layers and tightly coupled them in order to gain more data throughput. Fundamentally, this has not changed in over twenty years; the network stack has become a "sacred cow" of sorts – it is tweaked here and there from time to time (TCP Reno, New Reno, IPv4 to IPv6), but in essence it remains unchanged.

In terms of the software layering patterns [1], the network stack is in reality layered in name only as most of the principles (encapsulation, reuse, exchangeability) of layering are violated. This type of "layered" architecture is stifling and diverting innovation into workarounds (cross layers) rather than addressing core problem.

As part of the EU IST project 4WARD, we are proposing a new architecture to address these shortcomings and adhere to the principles of layering allowing diversity and evolvability of network stacks. This proposed component-based architecture encapsulates functionality and enables the dynamic creation of network stacks through the use of contracts, which promote a plug-and-play architecture by augmenting a traditional command signature with semantics and metadata. Contracts [12] provide formal semantics to enable components to connect and use functionality of other components as they require it. This allows the designers to create the particular network stack that is required by the application, rather than having to use a single rigid network stack that does not meet the needs of different applications. It is possible to manage legacy stacks using this architecture by using component wrappers. The design of our architecture is inspired by the Distributed Interface-Oriented Architecture (DIOA, [3]) and is based on design patterns from [1, 2].

2 Component Based Architecture

The use of components is a proven means to realize reusable, extensible software. Component software enables modularity to be built into architectures, designs, and implementations [2]. Component software thus encourages the move from the current huge monolithic systems to modular structures that offer the benefits of enhanced adaptability, scalability, and maintainability.

There are similarities between Component-based and Service-based Architectures (CBA vs. SoA). In general, architectures describe subsystems and relationships between them. They are also seen as an artefact of the system's design activities. In a CBA, the subsystems are components while in SoA the subsystems are services. Ideally, an implementation of an SoA is a CBA. In our case, the difference between an SoA and the CBA is that we focus on the design and implementation of network stacks (at runtime tightly coupled components) rather than loosely coupled business services, as would be the case in an SoA. A component model specifies the set of design rules that must be obeyed by components. These design rules improve composability by removing a variety of source interface mismatches.

Our component framework is novel, in that it uses a collection of policies [14] and contracts [12] to govern the interaction of components plugged into the framework. It enforces the more vital rules of interaction by encapsulating the required interaction mechanisms.

2.1 Components

A component encapsulates its constituent features as a unit of independent deployment. Thus, a component needs to be concretely separated from its environment and other components. As a unit of deployment, a component cannot be partially deployed. In this context, a third party cannot be expected to have access to the construction details of all the components involved.

A component is designed to be used for third party composition. Thus, it needs to be self-contained, and provide clear specifications of what it requires and what it provides. Hence, it has no externally observable state. It also needs to encapsulate its implementation and interact with its environment by means of well-defined interfaces. We use contracts for these purposes.

The functionality of a component is provided by reusable, modular building blocks. The component acts as an intelligent container in which the building blocks are assembled to provide the overall required functionality.

Core to the concept of components is the separation of interface, contracts, and implementation, which is also known as information hiding [5]. The interface and contract together specify the public parts of a component, enabling its implementation to be hidden. A component provides contract(s) via a component specification at analysis-design time. These contracts are refined into an implementation of that component at design-build time. Of course, a component can have many different implementations that can satisfy a given component specification; how a component is implemented internally is irrelevant at design time. At deployment time, the relevant implementation is used to satisfy deployment constraints.

2.2 Contracts

A contract is the unit of interoperability [12]. It represents the metadata and specification of semantics that is attached to an interface that mutually binds consumers and providers (implementers) of that interface. Contracts can cover functional and non-functional aspects. Functional aspects include the syntax and semantics of an interface. Non-functional aspects include quality-of-service, security, availability, and service level guarantees.

The purpose of a contract is to enable information to be shared between components. This includes information and the definition of how all types of data and knowledge is shared, including services, resources, and the behavior that is expected when one component participates in a contract with another component. This inter-component behavior is expressed by a set of obligations and benefits. Implementation-wise, this includes the registration, execution of functionality, and data exchange that takes place.

Furthermore, a contract describes the abstract services provided by a component. The primary goal of a contract is to guarantee interoperability between components. Interoperability refers to the ability of components to collaborate with each other, assuming compatibility not only of their interfaces but also of their run-time behavior and non-functional properties. A contract is composed of the following three parts: a) visibility models, b) protocol models, and c) non-functional specifications. Within 4WARD, we concentrate on Quality-of-Service (QoS) interfaces as an example.

The visibility model provides governance of an interface using policies to define the accessibility of the individual interface signatures. This effectively allows the dynamic definition of an interface into functional subsets.

The protocol model states the protocol dependencies between individual signatures in order to avoid run-time interoperability conflicts. Protocol dependence refers to: (1) a logical dependence affecting the availability of signatures according to prior calls to signatures, or (2) a required ordering of signatures. This implies that protocol dependencies restrict or stipulate the sequences in which the functionality of an interface can be called. Some formal notations for protocol specification include: Finite State Machines [6], Petri Nets [7], and Process Calculi [4].

Non-functional attributes are properties that govern or restrict the operation of the functionality specified by the contract, and include properties such as QoS, reliability, performance and availability. Quality interface models are concerned with functionality that is observable and/or measurable. In some cases, the metric specified can only be observed and is not measured (e.g., a client couldn't hear the caller well); other times, the measurement can be either fuzzy in nature (high, medium, low) or a computed or read value. Some languages for the specification and modeling of these properties include QML [8] and SML [9].

The association of a contract with an interface provides an externally visible and formal set of semantics of an interface. The contract provides a façade that specifies characteristics and behavior of interfaces in a formal manner.

2.3 Other Key Concepts

Interface	An interface is a list of signatures. A signature describes an abstract function, which may be either offered or required to access functionality. Signatures typically encompass the following elements: name, return type, ordered list of parameters with types, (optionally) set of possibly thrown exceptions.
Functional Block	Functional blocks are atomic units of functionality. They are combined to provide the overall functionality that is offered by a component. In general, a functional block generates, consumes, processes, and forwards information. This functionality is made available via a set of components through one or more contracts.
Policy	Policy is the unit of governance which can be applied within the framework. Formally, policy is a set of rules that are used to manage and control the changing and/or maintaining of the state of one or more managed entities [14].

Framework Communication Block	This specific functional block provides a common communication contract with the framework. Each component of the same framework must implement this functional block. It provides access to framework functionality for all the members of the framework via a common communications vehicle. The framework communication block may also contain groups of policy that is executed during any interaction with the framework services. This provides a mechanism to manage and control the behavior of a framework artifact (functional block, component, federation of components, component node).
Component Stack	A component stack is a group of hierarchically layered components. It can be used to create groupings of components within a component node. This allows the labeling of common groups of components e.g. (TCP/IP Stack).
Component Node	A component node is the foundation for components to be installed and execute on. It includes at least an execution environment, but typically adds a collection of services. It organizes the hosting of deployed components, and represents the nodes that the components exist on. A deployed component belongs to one and only one component node, but a component node can have many components (and component stacks) present on it. A group of component nodes forms a component node network.
Federation of Components	A federation is a union comprising a number of partially self-governing components united in a way (e.g., through majority voting, negotiation, or a floating leader) defined by one or more policies of the federation. The federation can provide a set of contracts for its constituent components, which presents a unified view of the functionality of the federation. The functionality offered by a federation of components may be distributed across many component node networks and is bound by both the components and the network communication channels between them.

2.4 Advantages of a Component-Based Architecture

A component-based architecture has the following advantages over the existing, traditional approach of monolithic/vendor specific system development, including:

1. *Supply of components from multiple sources* - This helps to prevent vendor lock-out or lock-in. It also allows a marketplace for components to exist; the selection of a component can include financial or quality considerations to be taken into account when selecting a component.
2. *Re-use of components* - Components may be re-used across multiple scenarios. In addition, new scenarios can often be seen as incremental changes to existing solutions. This addresses controlling additional cost when replacing or extending components to support new scenarios.

3. *Legacy System Support* - It may be necessary to bring legacy systems into a component-based architecture. This can be achieved by creating component facades between the legacy system and the existing components.
4. *Flexibility* - Since new services and products are delivered through the linking of components, this more flexible environment will allow a more diverse range of service products to be provided to customers.
5. *Validation* - Using the component framework, it will be possible to validate the deployed components via models at design time. A modeling tool can allow easy configuration of the components on a per component node and component node network basis. This configuration can be validated prior to deployment, as it is configured within the modeling tool.
6. *Traceability* - Traceability records the status changes of an artifact that is part of a system [13]. Traceability information can improve the control of software quality, development processes and deployed systems. Using component specifications (and associated contracts) throughout the lifecycle (analysis, design, development and deployment), it is possible to construct and integrate traceability maps [10] within the architecture. Traceability maps allow end-to-end lifecycle traceability while keeping a linkage to the traditional functional programming interfaces.

An important advantage of our component framework is that if a problem is uncovered within a system, it can only mean one of two things – a contract has been violated (development time) or the contract itself is incorrect (design time).

3 Infrastructure

3.1 Framework Services

The component framework has to provide the following core services in order to provide a viable component node upon which the component-based architecture can exist. These services can themselves be provided as system components within the framework:

- *Naming Service* - The naming service is responsible for generating and resolving unique names for the various entities (components, contracts, and contract instances) contained within the repository. The naming service interacts with the registration service when an entity initially registers with the system in order to assign that entity a unique object identifier.
- *Location Service* - A location service provides a means to map a request for an object to a particular instance of that object. Location services are typically built on top of naming services.
- *Registration Service* - A registration service provides a mechanism to identify and invoke the entity being registered. The information contained within the repository includes details on where (Components, Contracts and Contract instances) are located and how they can be accessed and/or invoked.
- *Repository Service* - The repository service provides access to the information that is contained within the system repository.

- *Naming Service* - The naming service is responsible for generating and resolving unique names for the various entities (components, contracts, and contract instances) contained within the repository. The naming service interacts with the registration service when an entity initially registers with the system in order to assign that entity a unique object identifier.
- *Policy Service* - The policy service acts as a supervisor of policies being carried out by all entities controlled by the system repository. The policy service orchestrates system and component functionality.
- *Security Service* - The security service ensures that only entities with proper permission can access entities that have provided corresponding access rights.

3.2 System Repository

The system repository is a data store for holding and managing information about the system and its constituent components. Information stored within the repository includes: component specifications, component implementation information, contract information, component instance information, polices, security and shared information. The repository itself is usually distributed in nature. The framework services interacts with the system repository to perform their specific functions.

3.3 Domains

A domain is an instance of a component-based platform that consists of a system repository and framework services as well as the members of the domain. A domain is a collection of entities that share a common purpose. Multiple independent domains can exist and can interact with each other via peering relationships (defined by contracts) at the domain borders.

4 Architecture Methodology

Figure 1 highlights the differing roles within the architecture, the overlap of toolsets, and the separation of concerns. There are three roles: designer, developer and deployer.

The *Designer* uses the modeling tools to construct new services from components. A designer operates in a world of models and component specifications. A designer can use existing component specifications or create new ones that will be implemented by a developer. A designer is typically a domain expert within the enterprise.

A *Developer* uses development tools to implement new and edit existing components. A developer can implement components based on a component specification, or generate a component specification from a new implementation of functionality. A developer is a domain expert in the particular implementation language or platform being used. A developer does not necessarily require domain knowledge of the business (designer) or the deployment infrastructure (deployer). A developer may produce implementations for a component marketplace and not actually be a member of the enterprise using the implementation produced. A

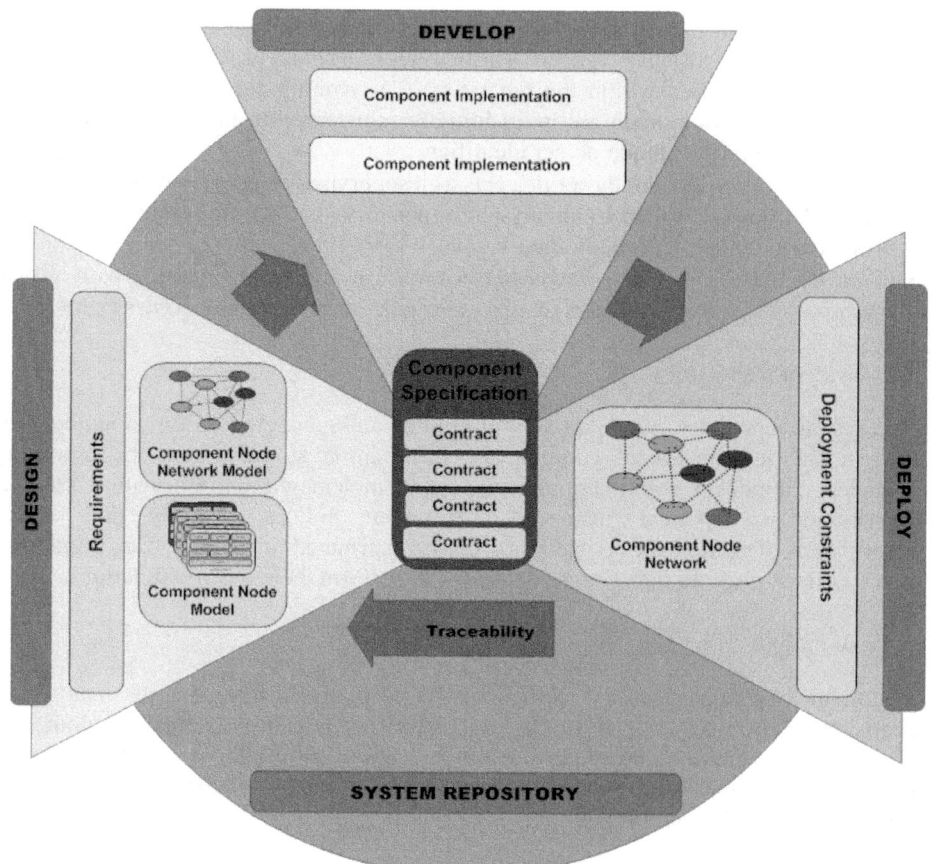

Fig. 1. CBA Methodology

developer role need not exist within an enterprise, as component implementations can be purchased from existing component vendors or a component marketplace.

A *Deployer* uses a model produced by the designer as a blueprint of the system to be built. A deployer selects the implementations of the required components based on deployment constraints and then instantiates these component implementations to create the specified system. A deployer is a domain expert within the area of the execution platform and infrastructure owned by the enterprise.

5 Enabling Design Time

The framework provides more structure and specification around software entities by encapsulating them into components with functional blocks described using component specifications; contracts are used to specify externally visible signatures. This structure enables moving to a model-driven design methodology using off the shelf components. The modeling tool can interact with the system repository to use the component specifications to validate links between the components within the model. The designer only deals with the component specification (i.e., the encapsulated contract(s) of a given component) and should never be required to have any knowledge of the implementation of the component. This clear separation of concerns is a critical feature of our approach.

Within 4WARD, we have been using a modeling tool (Meta-Edit) that allows us to create domain specific models that shape the problem and solution. We have used a component-based architecture to organize the software elements that provide the required functionalities within the nodes and the network.

The component node network model allows the configuration of the component nodes that are present in our network and the communication links between them. These models verify linkages between the nodes and alert the designer when a change to the model breaks a link by representing a component node as a component node model. Similarly, a component can be represented by a component model.

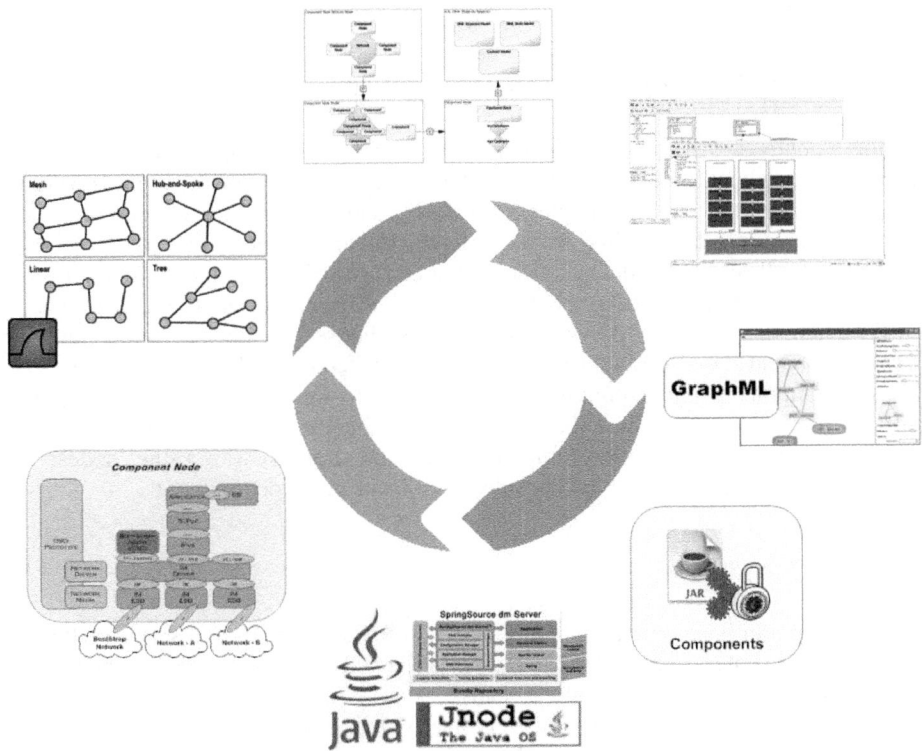

Fig. 2. Development and Deployment Cycle

The upper right part of figure 2 shows a diagram of a component node network model in which a number of component nodes have been created and interconnected. The communication links (connections) validate both sides of the connection to enforce communication compatibility (e.g., verify whether a chosen medium is available or not). If a problem is detected, it is highlighted to emphasize the problem. The nodes themselves are color-coded with respect to their location within the network. Green nodes represent consumer premises equipment, pink nodes are access points, yellow links are routers, and grey nodes indicate internet domain borders. Each node can be selected and further decomposed into its component node model to see its components. A component node also contains a listing of the available physical connection types available (e.g., Ethernet and WiFi). Furthermore, the appropriate component for these physical connections is automatically propagated into the component node model as a basis to start the component node configuration.

The modeling tool interacts with the system repository to provide a list of existing components that are available for use within the model tool. These components can then be linked to each other using the available contracts as units of interoperability.

A contract automatically validates a link: if both sides have an equivalent contract, then it is possible to create a valid linkage. This comparison is performed every time the model is changed or when the metamodel is changed. If a link becomes invalid, it is immediately highlighted within the model.

6   Enabling Development and Deployment

While a contract will allow us to check interoperability at a model level, additional constraints apply at both development and deployment time. Development constraints choose the implementation language, platform, and programming facilities used to implement a component. This allows different implementations to exist for a given component, all of which adhere to the component specification, but provide different cost-implementation tradeoffs or compliance with different technology constraints.

At deployment time, deployment constraints choose the required implementation of a component based on other criteria, such as different hardware/middleware. The chosen component implementations are then used to satisfy the required component specification from the design phase. The overall specification of the network, nodes present within the network, component implementations within the nodes; and federation of components can be considered a blueprint for deployment.

7   Legacy Systems

A legacy system is an enterprise's heritage of software systems and services. It poses a dilemma for enterprises, in that it can be perceived as an obstacle to implementing new business processes; mainly because it is typically hard to adapt to new requirements. A legacy system also typically locks in business knowledge. The knowledge stored comprises not only explicit knowledge about processes, policies and data, but also tacit knowledge that is used to smooth daily operations. As a result, a disruption to a legacy system can have severe impact on the enterprise operation.

We recommend a non-invasive approach for the integration of legacy systems based on [11]. This requires the identification of the components and functionalities to be exposed by the legacy system and the policies that govern access and visibility to the exposed functionality. Component specifications are then generated to wrap the exposed functionality and implement this mandatory set of framework services. These are then implemented as component wrappers based on the component specifications. These component wrappers serve as a framework interface and an adapter between the framework and the legacy system.

8 Related Work for Contracts

Our work was inspired by the original Design by Contract concept of Bertrand Meyer [16] and the application of that concept within the NGOSS architecture [3,12], both originating in the 1990s. Contracts as an artifact have been widely used in software engineering since the introduction of the concept. Beside adding contract facility to programming languages (as in Eiffel, or asassertions and annotations), interesting work has been published on using the Design by Contract concept to model and test software systems. Gupta et al. [17] describes a practical approach for contract methods, using an object's annotated structural representation (based on a UML class diagram). Ramkarthik et al. [18] shows how Java contract code can be generated from a formal notation, in this case Object Z. Giese [19] developed an approach that "provides mechanism to achieve a higher degree of independence, to exclude implicit implementation dependencies and make requirements and the provided behavior of components more concrete". In his approach, behavior is handled by external specifications. With regard to the quality of a software system, Baudry et al. have developed quality criteria (such as robustness and diagnosability in [20]) and approaches for the detection of erroneous runtime states of executable contracts in [21]. The resulting quality parameter is called vigilance and allows measuring the impact of contracts on a software system. On a similar level of abstraction, Enselme et al. [22] studied the analysis of hidden dependencies and the interactions of contracts. Lohmann et al. [25] demonstrate how the concept of contract can be used on the level of modeling (as compared to code level) and how visual mechanisms can help in the design of robust executable contracts. Within communication systems, the NGOSS architecture has stimulated investigations and studies focusing on contracts. Liu et al. [23] have identified non-functional requirements for contract specifications, mainly focusing on quality management and product evaluation. The concept of contracts and the NGOSS meta-model have been adapted for peer-to-peer management systems in European efforts, such as [14]. We have been noted that our work is very similar to cfengine [26,27] and the promise theory [28], however our work is based on models such as the SID/DEN-ng and architectures such as NGOSS (both from the TM Forum) and FOCALE, all of which addressing specific needs of network management rather than computer configuration management.

9 Conclusion

This paper described the rationale and features of our component-based architecture, and showed how to apply software design patterns (such as the pattern for generating a layered architecture) to the development of networks, namely the Future Internet. The use of patterns allows for rapid composition of federated components, which then can be translated directly into the configuration of network stacks. This approach addresses the underlying problem of today's bottlenecks in communication networks: tightly coupled layers of protocols that prevent encapsulation, reuse and exchangeability. Our approach is inspired by the architectural concepts of a DIOA and contracts, which provide us with the flexibility we need to empower designers in creating network stacks they need (as opposed by today's situation were all designers have to use the stacks provided and the only workaround is cross-layering). We have used the basic definitions discussed in this paper to define a modeling language, which in turn can be used to design and create flexible network stacks. The next step, which we are currently undertaking, is to automatically generate configurations from the editor and deploy them in a runtime environment to demonstrate our approach.

References

1. Buschmann, F., Meunier, R., Rohnert, H., Sommerlad, P., Stal, M.: Pattern-Oriented Software Architecture. A System of Patterns, vol. 1. Wiley, New York (1996)
2. Szyperski, C., Gruntz, D., Murer, S.: Component Software: Beyond Object-Oriented Programming, 2nd edn. Addison-Wesley, Boston (2002)
3. TMF: NGOSS Technological Neutral Architecture. TM Forum: TMF053, Ed. NGOSS Release 6.0, TNA Release 6.0, Version 5.6 (October 2005)
4. Bracciali, A., Brogi, A., Canal, C.: Dynamically Adapting the Behavior of Software Components. In: Arbab, F., Talcott, C. (eds.) COORDINATION 2002. LNCS, vol. 2315, pp. 88–95. Springer, Heidelberg (2002)
5. Parnas, D.L.: On the Criteria to Be Used in Decomposing Systems into Modules. Communications of the ACM 15(12), 1053–1058
6. Holzmann, G.J.: Design and Validation of Computer Protocols. Prentice Hall, Englewood Cliffs
7. van der Aalst, W., et al.: Component-Based Software Architectures: A Framework Based on Inheritance of Behavior. Science of Computer Programming 42(2-3), 129–171
8. Frølund, S., Koistinen, J.: Quality-of-Service Specification in Distributed Object Systems. Technical Report HPL-98-159. Hewlett Packard, Software Technology Laboratory
9. Service Modeling Language, Version 1.1, http://www.w3.org/TR/sml/
10. van der Meer, S., Fleck II, J.: Traceability Maps: a Tool for Managing Software Artifacts. In: Proc. of 15th Workshop of the HP Software University Association, Marrakech, Morocco, June 22-25 (2008)
11. Mecella, M., Pernici, B.: Designing Wrapper Components for e-Services in Integrating Heterogeneous Systems. VLDB Journal 10(1), 2–15
12. TMF: NGOSS Architecture Technology Neutral Specification - Contract Description: Business and System Views. TMF053B, Ed. TNA Release 6.3, Version 5.1 (November 2006)
13. van der Meer, S., et al.: Manageability of Autonomic Software Artifacts using Contracts and Traceability. In: Proc. of 2nd IEEE International Workshop on Modelling Autonomic Communications Environments (MACE 2007), San José, USA, October 29-30 (2007)
14. Strassner, J.: Policy Based Network Management. Morgan Kaufmann, San Francisco, ISBN 1-55860-859-1
15. Day, J.: Patterns in Network Architecture. Prentice Hall, Englewood Cliffs, ISBN 0-132-25242-2
16. Meyer, B.: Applying Design by Contract. IEEE Computer (1992)

17. Gupta, A., Raj, A.: Strengthening Method Contracts for Objects. In: APSEC (2006)
18. Ramkarthik, S., Zhang, C.: Generating Java Skeletal Code with Design Contracts from Specifications in a Subset of Object Z. In: ICIS COMSAR (2006)
19. Giese, H.: Contract – based Component System Design. In: ICSS (2000)
20. Baudry, B., le Traon, Y., Jézéquel, J.-M.:Robustness and Diagnosability of OO Systems Designed by Contracts. In: METRICS (2001)
21. le Traon, Y., Baudry, B., Jézéquel, J.-M.: Design by Contract to Improve Software Vigilance. IEEE Transactions on Software Engineering 32(8) (2006)
22. Enselme, D., Florin, G., Legond-Aubry, F.: Design by contracts Analysis of hidden dependencies in component based applications. Journal of Object Technology 3, 4 (2004)
23. Liu, X., et al.: Specification of Non-functional Requirements for Contract Specification in the NGOSS Framework for Quality Management and Product Evaluation. In: IEEE Fifth International Workshop on Software Quality, WoSQ 2007 (2007)
24. Carroll, R., Lehtihet, E., Fahy, C., van der Meer, S., Georgalas, N., Cleary, D.: Applying the P2P paradigm to management of large-scale distributed networks using a Model Driven Approach. In: 10th IEEE/IFIP NOMS 2006, Vancouver, Canada, April 3-7 (2006)
25. Lohmann, M., Sauer, S., Engels, G.: Executable_Visual_Contracts. In: 2005 IEEE Symposium on Visual Languages and Human-Centric Computing, VL/HCC (2005)
26. Burgess, M.: An Approach to Understanding Policy Based on Autonomy and Voluntary Cooperation. In: 16th IFIP/IEEE Distributed Systems: Operations and Management Barcelona, Spain, October 24-26 (2005)
27. cfengine: http://www.cfengine.org/
28. Bergstra, J., Burgess, M.: A static theory of promises (2010), http://project.iu.hio.no/papers/origin2.pdf (last accessed August 25, 2010)

Towards a Context-Aware Information Model for Provisioning and Managing Virtual Resources and Services

Yeongrak Choi[1], Jian Li[2], Yoonseon Han[1],
John Strassner[1], and James Won-Ki Hong[1,2]

[1] Division of IT Convergence Engineering, POSTECH, Pohang, Korea
[2] Dept. of Computer Science and Engineering, POSTECH, Pohang, Korea
{dkby,gunine,seon054,johns,jwkhong}@postech.ac.kr

Abstract. The demand for new and innovative services, and especially for personalized services, continues to increase. In such systems, different services may compete for the same set of shared resources. Hence, the *mix* of services and resources that each has often results in conflicting demands on shared resources, and is becoming increasingly difficult to manage. Autonomic systems that provide virtual resources and services can provide important management benefits to ensure that the needs of different services can simultaneously be met. This paper describes the requirements for provisioning and managing virtual resources and services, and extends the DEN-ng information model to architect such systems.

Keywords: Information Model, Autonomic Systems, Provisioning, Virtual Resource Management, Service Management, Context Awareness.

1 Introduction

Information technology systems are getting more complicated to manage. This is caused by many factors, such as an increased number of technologies and the increased complexity of individual devices that are used. This paper is mainly concerned with one type of business complexity – the ability to manage different services that each has different needs and diverse business objectives. This places two demands on the network and server infrastructure: (1) how to accommodate the various needs of different services that are sharing the same resources, and (2) how to accommodate the increasing amount and diversity of management and operational information. For instance, personalized services aim to provide customers with services that are tailored to their tasks and needs. While this is attractive for customers, it places a significant management burden on the provider of such services, who must try to accommodate different variations of the same service that are delivered to different customers.

One way to achieve this is to utilize virtual resources to create personalized virtual services. Virtualization has many benefits. For example, it can isolate different machines and applications that have maintenance and security requirements,

R. Brennan, J. Fleck II, and S. van der Meer (Eds.): MACE 2010, LNCS 6473, pp. 100–112, 2010.

decoupling hardware, operating system, and application dependencies. It can simultaneously provide availability, reliability, and backup policies that are targeted to the needs of different (and possibly isolated) machines and applications [15] [16]. By dynamically allocating the resources of physical servers among different applications, the business requirements of different applications can be met. However, virtualization technologies demand careful management. In order to use virtualization technologies effectively, policy management can be used to define which applications receive which virtual resources.

FOCALE [1] is a novel autonomic architecture for providing *context-aware* policy management [2]. In this approach, context is used to select the applicable working set of policy rules that are applicable for a given context; these policy rules are used to govern services and resources offered by the system being managed. This enables FOCALE to select new policy rules to govern the system (if appropriate). FOCALE uses separate maintenance and adjustment control loops to manage functionality. FOCALE uses the DEN-ng information model [3] to define context and policy management [4]. In this approach, knowledge from models is augmented with knowledge from ontologies to capture semantics and better understand the behavior of entities in the system through machine-based learning and reasoning.

Our modeling approach intends to fill the gap between managing virtual resources and the autonomic architecture to provide personalized services. When diverse applications, which are used to run personalized services, are running on our autonomic architecture, virtualization technologies simplify the actions of matching applications to available resources. Our model also addresses the investigation of the link between virtual resources and their services. In cloud computing, Infrastructure as a Service (IaaS) provides accessibility to a set of virtual resources that are tightly coupled to a given service, which can be used to form a building block to implement personalized services [17].

This paper focuses on extending the DEN-ng information model for representing and managing the provisioning of virtual and non-virtual heterogeneous resources and the services that they support. In provisioning, this model helps to decrease the effort of configuring the corresponding virtual and non-virtual resources; this in turn simplifies defining, deploying, and managing services. Moreover, this model shows how to reduce management complexity by providing unified management mechanisms for both virtual and non-virtual resources. This enables the existing model objects in DEN-ng, such as objects that represent the roles of people and devices, to be used to manage virtual as well as non-virtual resources and services.

The organization of the paper is as follows. Section 2 addresses key modeling requirements of virtual resources and services provisioning and management to provide personalized services. Section 3 explains the enhancements made to the original DEN-ng 7.0 model. Section 4 presents a use case which describes the applicability of our proposed model. Section 5 describes related work, and Section 6 discusses conclusions and future work.

2   Modeling Requirements for Provisioning and Management

In this paper, we define "provisioning" as a set of processes to deliver services (and optionally, resources) to customers according to certain service level agreements. The

Information Technology Infrastructure Library (ITIL) [5] and the enhanced Telecom Operations Map (eTOM) [6] define high-level "best practices" that describe processes and process workflows that include provisioning and related functions; however, they do not describe lower-level aspects of how to provision infrastructure components. The ITIL and eTOM documents are inherently high-level because different organizations use different business processes and workflows to accomplish the same task. This can be remedied by defining a common set of objects to represent concepts corresponding to different concerns, ranging from business concepts such as Service Level Agreements (SLAs) to network concepts such as protocols and device configurations. The OMG's Model Driven Architecture (MDA) initiative [7] can be used to define and generate code for the different objects required to create, deploy, and manage the provisioning process. This results in the following key requirements that an information model must satisfy to achieve this.

An information model must be able to represent entities in an extensible manner. The use of software patterns [8], such as the role-object pattern [9] and the policy management pattern [3], can be used to provide an extensible framework that can represent these and other variations while avoiding class explosion.

An information model must be able to clearly differentiate between entities and metadata that can describe various aspects and behavior of a managed entity.

An information model should be able to represent various policy rules for governing system operation. Typically, many policy rules will be applicable to a given situation; hence, it is critical to select the correct set of policy rules for a given context in order to define appropriate system behavior and services. A very powerful mechanism for doing this is to use context to select the set of policy rules that are applicable at a given point in time.

3   Design of the Enhanced DEN-ng Information Model

This section defines extensions to the DEN-ng 7.0 information model that define a more flexible and feature-rich approach for representing provisioning and managing virtual and non-virtual resources and services. This paper describes specific extensions to the Resource domain, which is part of a larger effort to represent and manage virtualization technologies.

3.1   Introduction of VirtualResource into the DEN-ng Model

Fig. 1 illustrates our extension of the Resource domain of DEN-ng to accommodate virtualization. We used the following three steps to develop this extension: 1) define a set of initial classes using applicable software patterns, 2) extend this model by connecting elements in this model to applicable parts of the rest of the DEN-ng model, and 3) represent the complex interaction between resources and other important entities specifically for provisioning.

In order to model virtual resources in a technology-neutral way, we decided to build our model based on the existing DEN-ng information model. In DEN-ng 7.0, the definition of a resource was: "A physical and/or logical entity that is of interest to the managed environment". The DEN-ng 7.0 Resource class had three subclasses: PhysicalResource (i.e., an object that you can pick up and hold), LogicalResource (i.e., objects that cannot be picked up and held), and CompoundResource, which enables managed entities to have both physical and logical resource characteristics and behavior (e.g., a node in a topology diagram that has physical and logical components).

To maintain compatibility with the existing DEN-ng model, we defined a model for virtual resources with the following changes. First, we changed the hierarchy of Resource to include the VirtualResource and NonVirtualResource subclasses. Second, we changed the definition of Resource to encompass both of these two subclasses; its new definition is: "A Resource is any virtual or non-virtual component or system. A Resource contains a set of physical and/or virtual entities that are of interest to the managed environment. A Resource may represent a limited or critical entity that is required by other entities." Third, we used the original DEN-ng definition of Resource as the new definition of NonVirtualResource, and moved the original Resource hierarchies under NonVirtualResource. Fourth, we made a new definition for VirtualResource, which is: "A VirtualResource is an abstraction that decouples the physical manifestation of a Resource from its logical operation". Note that we are ignoring for the moment the experimental definition of virtual resource present in this version of DEN-ng; this version was built by the AutoI FP7 team [10], and will be discussed further in section 4. Finally, we are ignoring CompoundResource for the sake of simplicity.

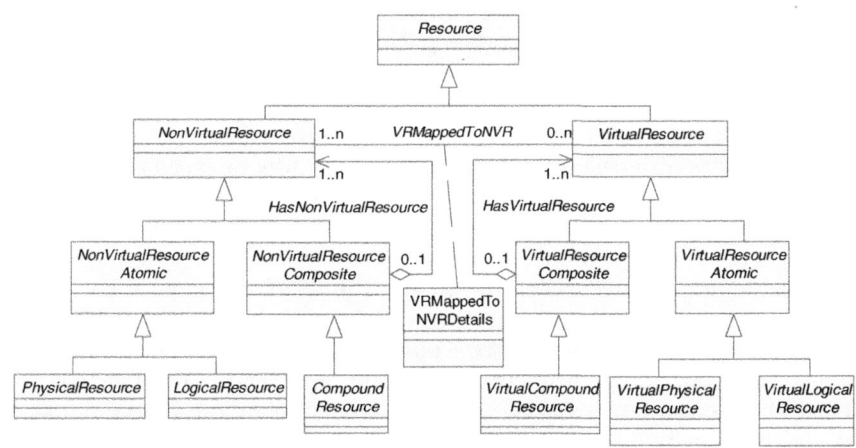

Fig. 1. Modified Top-level Resource Model

Now, we add an association between NonVirtualResource and VirtualResource, which models the dependency that VirtualResources have on their non-virtual hosts. This is shown in Fig. 1. The composite pattern is a powerful and extensible way to define graph and tree structures that represent part-whole hierarchies [8]. The inherent extensibility that the composite pattern provides implies that it can also be applied to the NonVirtualResource hierarchy to enhance its functionality. Therefore, we apply the composite pattern to both VirtualResource and NonVirtualResource, as shown in Fig. 1.

When we apply the composite pattern to the original (now non-virtual) Resource, we need to move its original three subclasses (PhysicalResource, LogicalResource, and CompoundResource) to one of the new subclasses introduced by the composite pattern. Both PhysicalResource and LogicalResource can be atomic classes, whereas CompoundResource is inherently composite (because it contains at least one physical and at least one logical Resource). Therefore, we make PhysicalResource and LogicalResource subclasses of NonVirtualResourceAtomic, and CompoundResource a subclass of NonVirtualResourceComposite, as shown in Fig. 1. Note that VirtualPhysicalResource was modeled as a subclass of VirtualResourceAtomic. This class represents the physical concepts of a Resource that has been virtualized (e.g., virtualized CPU, memory, hard-disk, and etc.). In addition, it describes different types of virtual hardware that constitutes a virtual product.

3.2 Management Using Context-Aware Policy Rules

We have introduced the VRMappedToNVR association, which models the dependency between a NonVirtualResource and the set of VirtualResources that are created from it. However, the interaction between these two different types of Resources is very complex, and additional classes and relationships must be introduced in order to properly model its semantics. Moreover, modeling the interaction without proper patterns may highly constrain its scalability as well. In order to solve these two problems, we utilized the policy pattern [2] [3].

Fig. 2 illustrates how context-aware policies are used to manage subclasses of VirtualResources. In Fig. 2, the policy pattern avoids various anti-patterns as well as a tendency to represent policy rules as "special cases" that cannot be shared or reused. Since various policy rules could be applied to govern how virtual resources are created and managed, a pattern is a particularly useful way to model this feature, since it provides a template for implementing a reusable solution to a commonly occurring design problem. By applying the policy pattern, we not only separate the representation of policy from its content, but we enable the semantics of the association to be adjusted according to the nature of the policy. By adding an association from PolicyRuleStructure to VRMappedToNVRDetails, policy related DEN-ng classes such as PolicyRuleStructure (this is the superclass of different types of policy rules, including event-condition-action, goal, and utility function policies [3]) and ManagementPolicy (this is the superclass of policy rules that are bound to a particular target entity [3]) can be used to define policy rules in an extensible fashion [2]. For example, different metadata can be applied to different types of policy rules to ensure that they are applied to specific types of managed entities.

Policy rules can then be associated with context to change the governance mechanisms in accordance with changes in context. In DEN-ng, context is modeled using two main classes: Context and ContextData. The latter represents different aspects of context, while the former represents a complete aggregate of context aspects that together represent a complete whole. For example, a virtual service may be made supported by different virtual devices; the set of resources that each virtual device provides would be a collection of ContextData, and the virtual service would be modeled by Context.

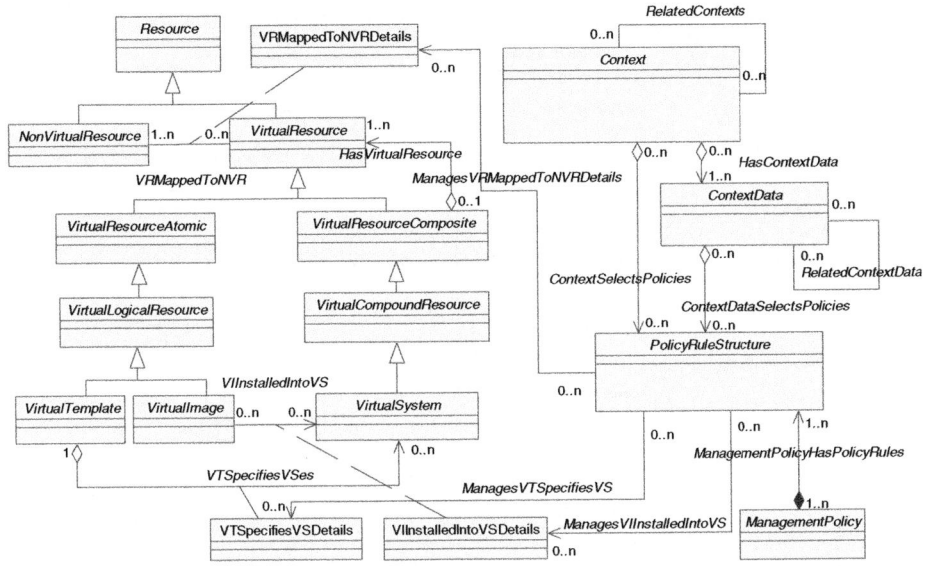

Fig. 2. The Use of Context-Aware Policies for Managing VirtualResource Subclasses

The basic DEN-ng loop uses Context and ContextData to select the appropriate set of policy rules to realize the set of governance operations required. Policy rules select roles that entities play; this is used to define functionality as well as to define the set of management and operational data that should be monitored by the control loop. Hence, context changes can be detected by changes in the state of the entities being managed; this (as well as other context changes) is used to adjust the policy rules that are used to define the services and resources that are offered at any given time.

3.3   Interacting PersonRole with VirtualResources

Fig. 3 shows the interaction of PersonRole and the subclasses of VirtualResources, such as VirtualTemplate, VirtualImage and VirtualSystem. Note that several classes and associations are not shown to make this figure easier to read.

The PersonRole concept is reused in its entirety from DEN-ng, which has a rich model for representing different types of interactions between people, devices, and services. We extended the concept of VirtualResource to support provisioning virtual environments using the VirtualSystem, VirtualImage, ImageRepository, VirtualTemplate, and TemplateRepository classes and their subclasses.

A VirtualSystem (VS) is a software implementation of a system, such as a computer, that contains PhysicalResources as well as LogicalResources. In this model, we modeled the VirtualSystem as a subclass of VirtualCompoundResource, because this concept must contain both VirtualPhysicalResources and VirtualLogicalResources.

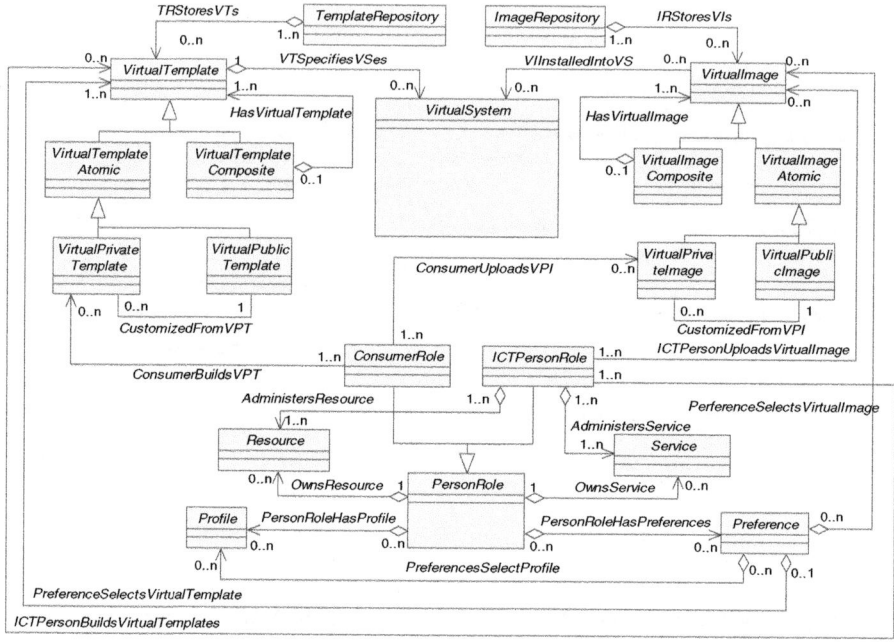

Fig. 3. Interaction between VirtualImage, VirtualTemplate and PersonRole

A VirtualImage (VI) is a file on a physical disk that is interpreted by a Virtual Machine Monitor (which is also known as a Hypervisor) as a repository [11]. The VirtualImage holds the file system where the OS will run from. VMMs enable multiple OSs to run concurrently on a host computer.

A VirtualTemplate (VT) is a virtual hardware specification and configuration description of a VirtualSystem. A VirtualTemplate may contain meta information that helps a VMM to generate a VirtualSystem, such as: 1) type of processors to be assigned to the VS, 2) the amount of memory the VS requires, 3) the location of the VI that contains the OS that runs on the VS, 4) virtual IP and MAC addresses to be assigned to the VS, and 5) other information that might be used for billing or other purposes.

There are an important set of associations between VIs and PersonRoles as well as between VTs and PersonRoles. A virtual *public* template (or image) is a VT (or VI) that is defined by an administrator for use by different types of ConsumerRoles. In contrast, a virtual *private* template (or image) is a VT (or VI) that has been personalized to suit the needs of a specific ConsumerRole. The full model realizes the CustomizedFromVPT (and the CustomizedFromVPI) associations as association classes, and then uses the policy pattern in a manner similar to that explained in the previous section to govern which set of policy rules control which set of changes a given ConsumerRole can make to a public VT (or VI).

VirtualImages may contain other VirtualImages; the same applies to VirtualTemplates. We used the composite pattern to model the creation of hierarchies of configurations for both VIs and VTs.

A PersonRole represents the part played by a Person in a given context. This includes the definition of any appropriate characteristics and behavior that it entails. There are two main types of PersonRoles: (1) ICTPersonRole and (2) ConsumerRole. ICTPersonRole represents PersonRoles that are involved in the design, development, management, and maintenance of information and communication technologies. ConsumerRole represents PersonRoles that can use, consume, or subscribe to Products, Services, and Resources. Since the roles for ICTPersonRole and ConsumerRole are different, their relationship with VirtualTemplates and VirtualImages are different. We use the role-object pattern, which enables a component object to be adapted to different needs through transparently attached role objects [8] [9], to represent these differences. This pattern is especially useful in separating the intrinsic and contextual characteristics and behavior of an entity. For example, ICTPersonRole could have been granted all privileges on building VirtualTemplates and VirtualImages no matter whether they are public or private; in contrast, ConsumerRole only has the permission to build his own private VirtualTemplate and VirtualImage. The use of private VirtualTemplates and VirtualImages enables the service configuration to be customizable according to Customers profiles and preferences.

3.4 Providing Services with VirtualResources

VirtualResources also play a key role of supporting the delivery of Services. In the original DEN-ng, PhysicalResource and LogicalResource are associated with ResourceFacingService, an abstraction that defines the characteristics and behavior of a particular Service that is not directly seen or purchased by customers but is nevertheless required for the proper operation of the service. (This is in contrast with CustomerFacingService, which is an abstraction that defines the characteristics and behavior of a particular Service that a customer purchases, leases, uses and/or is directly aware of in some other way). Similarly, VirtualResources are also associated with ResourceFacingServices.

Fig. 4 illustrates how the subclasses of VirtualResources are associated with ResourceFacingServices. The aggregation VPRHostsRFS defines the set of VirtualPhysicalResources that are required for this particular ResourceFacingService to function correctly. This is a *passive* relationship, and is used primarily to define which PhysicalResources are required to host a given service. The VLRImplementsRFS aggregation defines the set of VirtualLogicalResources that are required for the particular ResourceFacingService to function correctly. This is an *active* relationship, and defines the set of LogicalResources that are required to enable a ResourceFacingService to function. With these two aggregations, this information model can represent how a VirtualSystem hosts and implements a ResourceFacingService, because its super class VirtualCompoundResource is composed of a set of VirtualPhysicalResources and VirtualLogicalResources.

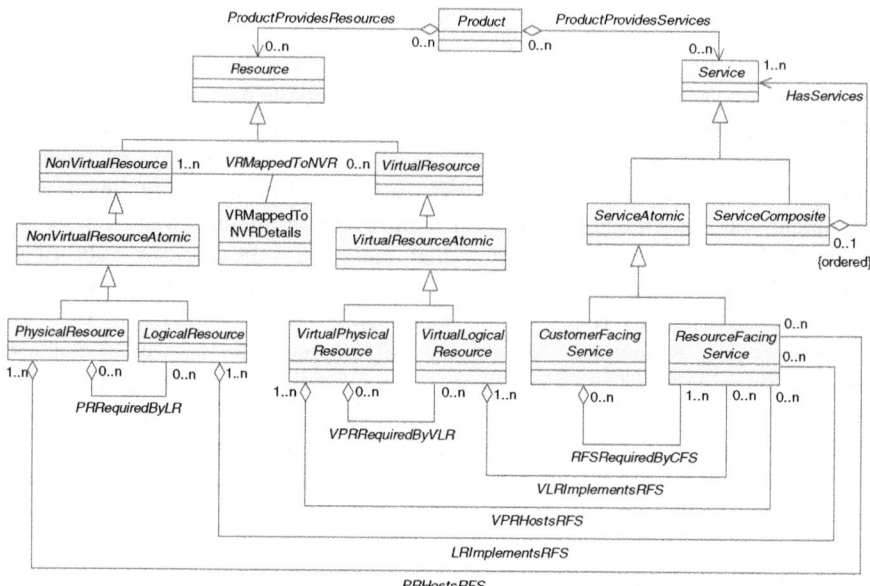

Fig. 4. Interactions between Services and VirtualResources

4 Applicability to SLA-Aware Services with Virtual Resources

The use case scenario depicted for the applicability of the proposed model presents the ability to satisfy the need of personalized services with virtual resources that are governed by one or more service level agreements. The scenario demonstrates how the contracts between a provider and the user of personalized services are not violated when virtual resources are provisioned and delivered into customers.

In DEN-ng, a service level agreement (SLA) is defined as a type of agreement that represents a formal negotiated agreement between two parties designed to create a common understanding about products, services, priorities, responsibilities and so forth. An SLA is one way to define the service level that is expected for a service, and can thus be used for personalized services as well. A DEN-ng SLA specifies a set of appropriate procedures and target metrics between parties to achieve and maintain specified goals, such as Quality of Service. However, it is difficult to reflect the characteristics of both non-virtual and virtual resources responding to personalized services into a contract. Although virtualization has interoperability advantages by abstracting the physical details of heterogeneous resources, some SLA statements may need to refer to specific resources. In addition, SLA terms are interpreted differently for different contexts. For example, when the security level is described for providing a personalized service, the context of the person is critical. The same person may be involved in tasks that have very different security requirements (e.g., work vs. entertainment). In addition, individuals will have different privacy requirements that are again influenced by context. To address these problems, our

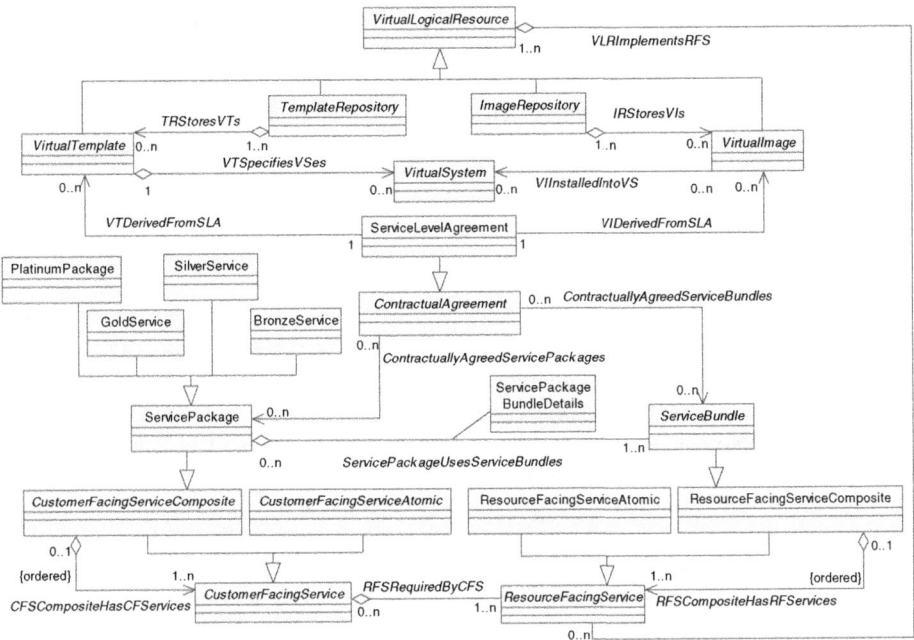

Fig. 5. Providing SLA-aware personalized services with virtual resources

modeling approach helps to identify items and functions and relate them to virtual and non-virtual resources, and then define how both are mapped to the same SLA.

Fig. 5 addresses how this use case can be applied using our proposed model when a VirtualSystem is provisioned based on VirtualTemplates and VirtualImages. For providing personalized services, a provider can define a set of services, where each service has different characteristics for various user-specific applications. For instance, the provider can define four different concrete service classes, such as premium, gold, silver and bronze service, to describe unique aspects of different personalized services. These classes are subclasses of CustomerFacingService. VirtualTemplate and VirtualImage are used to provision the appropriate virtual logical resources for a particular set of services. In Fig. 5, the ServiceLevelAgreement class (which represents an SLA) is defined as a subclass of the ContractualAgreement class. VirtualTemplate and VirtualImage are generated in accordance with ServiceLevelAgreement by considering interests of both users and the provider. Contractual agreement details of the ServiceLevelAgreement are described using the ServicePackage and ServiceBundle classes. A ServiceBundle class represents a collection of specifications of ResourceFacingServices; each ResourceFacingService defines a particular *class of service* that in turn specifies the Quality of Service (QoS) that this ResourceFacingService should receive. Each ServiceBundle interacts with one or more VirtualLogicalResources. In contrast, a ServicePackage contains a set of applications that are to be collectively treated according to a given SLA, and uses a set of ServiceBundles (one for each application in the ServicePackage) to deliver the application-behavior required. For example, a GoldService user and a SilverService user may use the same application, but the QoS for the GoldService user will be higher than the QoS for the SilverService user. These relationships strengthen the provisioning of personalized services with virtual resources even when the contract is changed between the provider and customers. When there are modifications of an SLA due to the changes in business requirements or customer needs, the associations of SLA related classes can identify which changes should be applied to fulfill the contract.

5 Related Work

[3] provides a comparison of the DEN-ng, DMTF CIM [13], and TMF SID [14] models. There are five key reasons for choosing DEN-ng. First, the CIM and the SID do not have a context model, whereas DEN-ng has a well-developed context model. In network management, there will be hundreds of thousands of policies of different types (e.g., business, system, and device configuration); at any given time, most will not be applicable. Furthermore, as business needs and environmental conditions change, virtual resources and services need to change as well. Context is therefore critical for both selecting the set of policies that are applicable at any given time as well as determining the specific set of virtual resources and services required. Second, the CIM and the SID do not have a metadata model, whereas DEN-ng has a very well developed metadata model. This means that the CIM and the SID cannot differentiate between data that describes the intrinsic characteristics and behavior of a managed entity versus data that describes how that managed entity is used; this limits extensibility. Third, the CIM does not use software patterns, and the SID has only a small fraction of the patterns used in DEN-ng compared to DEN-ng. This also limits the extensibility of the model. Fourth, the CIM and the SID do not provide any mechanisms to orchestrate behavior, such as a finite state machine, which DEN-ng does provide. This is crucial, as it enables state and actions to be taken to be directly translated from the model into generated code. Finally, unlike the CIM and the SID, DEN-ng models an entity in a *holonic* fashion – as a complete entity as well as a collection of different aspects of an entity; this provides a powerful and extensible way to represent and manage behavior.

The AUTOI project [10] models the virtualization of network resources and services. The objective of the AUTOI project is to define a set of management overlays to control virtualized network resources and services defined by the mapping of business requirements to network functionality. The core idea is to use a common language in a machine-understandable form to orchestrate heterogeneous resources and services, and translate it to a set of Domain Specific Languages to control each actual resource and service. The AUTOI model uses an extension of the DEN-ng information model as the common language to capture and express all necessary concepts in the environments. The main benefit of the AUTOI model is a natural, continuous linkage and orchestration of business goals, virtual resources, and services. However, this model is limited in functionality and extensibility compared to the model described in this paper. Specifically, the VirtualResource class of AUTOI is defined as a subclass of Resource, which is not technically correct since it is not a Resource according to the DEN-ng definition of "resource". While relationships are defined between PhysicalResource and VirtualPhysicalResource (and similarly for their logical counterparts), these relationships are very high-level in nature and do not provide enough details to properly model the provisioning of virtualized services. Hence, our proposal would be to use the AutoI framework, but replace the existing AutoI model with our model.

6 Concluding Remarks

Although there have been many different virtual resources and services already deployed, managing these virtual resources and services is still a very complicated process. To our knowledge, no detailed model exists that can be used to provision and manage virtual resources and their services. This paper has briefly described such a model, and more importantly, has shown how it can be used to *personalize* services. Our modeling approach helps to represent virtual resources and their services by defining a set of classes and representing associations with software patterns, which provides inherent extensibility. For future work, we will continue to develop this model, and prototype how VirtualResources and VirtualServices are managed using ontologies and first order logic. The advantage of adding ontologies and first order logic is that in a manner similar to FOCALE, we could then treat data corresponding to the model as *facts* that could then be sent to the ontologies, where inferences could be produced using first order logic. Once this is done, we can realize a set of detailed network scenarios, deploy this model and its associated ontologies into the FOCALE architecture, and then prototype how managing VirtualResources and VirtualServices could be used for provisioning and managing more innovative and customized services with VirtualResources and VirtualServices.

Acknowledgments. This work was partly supported by the IT R&D program of MKE/KEIT [KI003594, Novel Study on Highly Manageable Network and Service Architecture for New Generation] and WCU (World Class University) program through the National Research Foundation of Korea funded by the Ministry of Education, Science and Technology (Project No. R31-2008-000-10100-0).

References

1. Strassner, J., Agoulmine, N., Lehtihet, E.: FOCALE – A Novel Autonomic Networking Architecture. International Transactions on Systems, Science, and Applications (ITSSA) Journal 3(1), 64–79 (2007)
2. Strassner, J., de Souza, J.N., Raymer, D., Samudrala, S., Davy, S., Barrett, K.: The Design of a Novel Context-Aware Policy Model to Support Machine-Based Learning and Reasoning. Journal of Cluster Computing 12(1), 17–43 (2009)
3. Strassner, J.: Introduction to DEN-ng, Tutorial for FP7 PanLab II Project, January 21 (2009),
   http://www.autonomic-communication.org/teaching/ais/
   slides/0809/Introduction_to_DEN-ng_for_PII.pdf
4. Strassner, J.: Based Network Management. Morgan Kaufman, San Francisco (2003)
5. ITIL, http://www.itil-officialsite.com/home/home.asp

6. TMF, eTOM,
   http://tmforum.org/BusinessProcessFramework/1647/home.html
7. OMG, MDA, http://www.omg.org/mda/
8. Gamma, E., Helm, R., Vlissides, J.: Design Patterns-Elements of Reusable Object-Oriented Software. Addison-Wesley, Reading (November 2000)
9. Bäumer, D., Riehle, D., Siberski, W., Wulf, M.: The Role Object Pattern,
   http://hillside.net/plop/plop97/Proceedings/riehle.pdf
10. AUTOI (Autonomic Internet, an FP7 project),
    http://ist-autoi.eu/autoi/index.php
11. OpenNebula,
    http://www.opennebula.org/documentation:documentation
12. Westerinen, A., Schnizlein, J., Strassner, J., Scherling, M., Quinn, B., Herzog, S., Huynh, A., Carlson, M., Perry, J., Waldbusser, S.: Terminology for Policy-Based Management. RFC3198 (November 2001)
13. DMTF, CIM Schema: Version 2.24,
    http://www.dmtf.org/standards/cim/cim_schema_v2240
14. TMF, SID Schema,
    http://tmforum.org/InformationFramework/1684/home.html
15. Federica (Federated E-infrastructure Dedicated to European Researchers Innovating in Computing network Architectures) project, http://www.fp7-federica.eu
16. Reservoir fp7 project, http://reservoir-fp7.eu/index.php
17. IAAS framework project, http://www.iaasframework.com

A Framework for Automated Fault Recovery Planning in Large-Scale Virtualized Infrastructures

Feng Liu[1], Vitalian A. Danciu[1], and Pavlo Kerestey[2]

[1] Munich Network Management Team,
Ludwig-Maximilians-Universität, München
{liufeng,danciu}@nm.ifi.lmu.de
[2] Technische Universität München
pkerestey@mytum.de

Abstract. Multi-layered provisioning architectures such as those in emergent virtualized (e.g. cloud) infrastructures exacerbate the cost of faults to a degree where automation effectively constitutes a prerequisite for operations. The acquisition of management information and the execution of routine tasks have been automated to some degree; however the decision processes behind fault management in large-scale environments have not. This paper addresses automation of such decision processes by proposing a planning-based fault recovery algorithm based on hierarchical task networks and data models for the knowledge necessary to the recovery process. We embed these concepts in a generic architecture and evaluate its prototypical implementation with respect to function and scalability.

Keywords: fault management, AI planning, virtualization, cloud computing.

1 Introduction

Fault management is indisputably a major management challenge for operators of large infrastructures such as in emergent large-scale infrastructures in cloud computing. Despite a high degree of system homogeneity in these infrastructures, fault management is hampered by sheer scale, as brought to attention by recent high profile incidents [11,1].

Host virtualization as a key technology in such installations further complicates matter by adding an extra layer of abstraction, an extra layer of software as well as the dissolution of traditional, fixed resource assignment. The involvement of highly skilled human operators limits the efficiency of the manual portions of recovery processes, requiring decision support concepts to control their work load and allow recovery solutions to be devised in a timely manner to minimise outage period. One general avenue of approach is the introduction of AI planning methods to organise recovery actions according to stored management knowledge.

We propose a solution based on a Hierarchical Task Network (HTN) planning algorithm as the core of a generic decision support system for fault recovery. The algorithm plans a recovery process by constantly selecting and refining high-level tasks into operational management actions according to knowledge on the state of the infrastructure, the inter-dependencies of components and applications, the potentially available management actions and their effects.

R. Brennan, J. Fleck II, and S. van der Meer (Eds.): MACE 2010, LNCS 6473, pp. 113–123, 2010.

We discuss the requirements on a recovery planning solution based on a cloud computing scenario in Section 2 and present the core algorithm, knowledge data models and an architecture for automated fault recovery in Section 3. Section 4 presents a performance evaluation of our prototypical implementation of the algorithm. We discuss related work in the domains of planning and fault management automation in Section 5.

2   Challenges and Requirement Analysis

We derive requirements on automated fault recovery from the challenges in cloud computing scenarios in the following.

2.1   Scenario

Figure 1 illustrates a typical setting of services being provisioned based on the PaaS (platform-as-a-service) model, as known from e.g. Google AppEngine, Heroku and the efforts toward data centre consolidation and re-centralisation. The PaaS/virtualization middleware maps physical resources to virtual service components. It also offers flexible allocation and deployment of virtual resources (e.g. VMs) for the hosted services and provides software stacks for the hosted IT services, e.g. applications, libraries, DB systems. Virtual machines are configured and provisioned as disposable service elements of the service platform. Figure 1 exemplifies two usage scenarios: the *Web App* providing dynamic web services based on service elements such as a load-balancer to normalise the network traffic during the peak time, a database for dynamic content and process units to serve HTTP requests, supported by cache elements to accelerate identical queries. Similarly, the *Stream App* provides a pipelined/staged process service relying on large numbers of processing elements governed by a load balancer and DB elements.

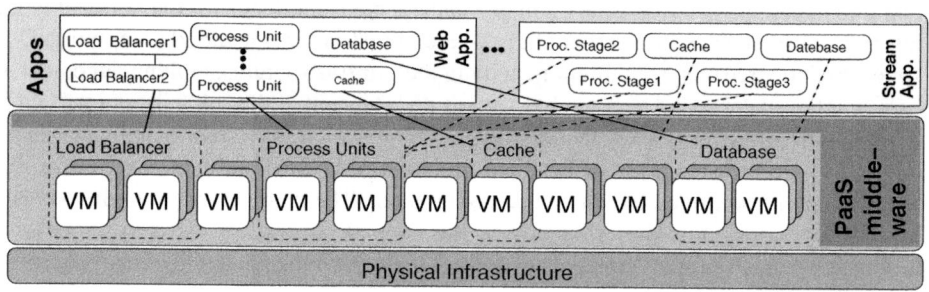

Fig. 1. PaaS Scenario

Faults can occur on all layers of this setup, in a *horizontal view*. Services are sustained by multitudinous components. Servers, storage, database and network components form complex interdependencies, in which a single faulty component could degrade or corrupt the whole service. In the scenario, a defected physical server could bring down VMs and deteriorate the associated services.

In a *vertical view*, multiple layers participate in service delivery. The stack of components across all layers increase the potential for faults with different characteristics, depending on the impacted layer. For instance, the corruption of the virtualization/middleware layer will impact the services running on top of it, even if the physical server remained intact. The multiple-layered architecture exacerbates the management challenges, as faults may be detected unpredictably on any layer, manifesting themselves in a range from sluggish response time to complete service interruption.

The rate of concurrent failure events in such a large-scale infrastructure overwhelm the operators due to high service density, operator-to-server ratio and growing customer expectations on reliability; thus, human-centric fault management is rendered all but infeasible. What is worse, time-critical and highly stressful fault recovery leads to an increased rate of human error both in terms of decisions as well as during the execution of management action.

2.2 Requirements

To meet the challenges posed by scenarios in large-scale environments, fault recovery must be timely and inexpensive (in terms of manual work), thus requiring the following:

- SCALABILITY. A fault management solution must be able to take into account high numbers of concurrent faults that impact a large number of customers operating large numbers of applications/services.
- SPEED. The time cost of recovery is a critical factor directly affecting users' experience of the service, as well as the financial penalties due in accordance with service level agreements. Hence, recovery planning must be done quickly.
- SERVICE DRIVEN OPERATION. Some services are more important than others, financially or technically. Thus, a recovery solution must take into account meta-information about services (e.g. maximum down-time before penalty), impacted users, available resources and so on. This information must be made available in a machine-readable form to enable recovery automation.
- DEPENDENCY AWARENESS. A failed component rarely disturbs only one application or service instance. In the same manner, a service type is rarely used by only one customer. Inter-dependencies existing between components must be taken into account to effectively allow a prioritisation of recovery tasks. Hence, a recovery solution must be able to exploit information about the inter-dependencies present in the infrastructure.
- ENCODING OF RECOVERY KNOWLEDGE. Fault recovery is a knowledge-intensive management task: information on the current state of a system and knowledge on how to treat particular faults must be available. A recovery approach must incorporate concepts to encode and use information about component interfaces, monitoring events, and partial states of infrastructure elements.

3 Approach

The proposed solution revolves around the architecture sketched in Figure 2, which incorporates a *planner* as the core component, as well as the information sources necessary to the recovery planning process, as stipulated by the requirements.

3.1   Components

The communication between the central planning system and the PaaS middleware is facilitated by monitoring and execution agents. The *monitoring agent* is responsible for collecting data and writing them into the *state database*, as well as triggering the planner if anomalies are detected. The *execution agent* implements selected management actions on the underlying infrastructure. The *knowledge database* contains two types of information: task descriptions (i.e. fault recovery recipes as either abstract or atomic actions) and system descriptions containing the dependencies between applications and virtual resources. Ideally, such information is obtained by discovery mechanisms; lacking that, it may be input by administrators.

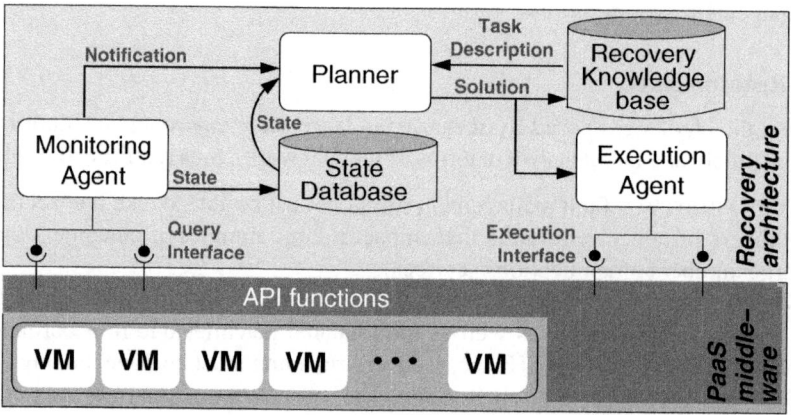

Fig. 2. Design of a planning-based recovery architecture

3.2   Recovery Process

Upon receiving a notification, the planner computes a set of solutions based on information retrieved from state database (current system status) and the knowledge database (corresponding task and system descriptions). The result is written back to the recovery knowledge base and saved as history data for documentation.

Once plans have been computed they may be examined by human administrators with respect to the feasibility and correctness. (To support such interaction, our prototype includes a web-based front end.) Finally a selected plan is enacted by the execution agents on the API of underlying middleware. The execution process is constantly supervised by the monitoring agent (in terms of partial state changes), which trigger re-planning in case of secondary faults or exceptions.

3.3   Planning Model and Knowledge Representation

Formally, a a planning problem has as input a set of actions, a state model of the system and a planning objective (goal)[12]. It produces one or more courses of actions that fulfil the goal.

Table 1. Information items and examples

Service information denotes semantics and dependencies of the services running on a virtual infrastructure. A Virtual Application is associated with one or more VM–Types.

```
                                    0..*
                        ┌─────────────────────────┐
              0..1      │ Virtual Machine Type     │
┌──────────────────┐    ├─────────────────────────┤
│ Virtual Application│   │ + String ID             │
├──────────────────┤    │ + Hash maxThreshold     │
│ + String ID      │    │ + List services         │
└──────────────────┘    │ + int amount            │
                        └─────────────────────────┘
"vApps":{
  "WebApp": {
    "procUnit":{
      "amount": 3,
      "clustered": "deny",
      "MAX_threshold":{
        "cpu": 95,
        "mem": 90,
        "hdd": 90, ... },
      "services":["app", "nginx"] },
    "database":{...},
    "loadbalancer:{...}" }   }
```

State information encodes the current status of the underlying infrastructures. Essential information such as CPU and memory utilization as well as available storage space taken by a VM are included as part of VM state information.

```
                      *      1 ┌──────────┐  *
┌─────────────────┐           │ State    │
│ Virtual Machine │           ├──────────┤
├─────────────────┤           │ + String ID│
│ + String ID     │           └──────────┘       1
│ + int CPU       │           ┌──────────┐
│ + int mem       │    *      │ Cluster  │
│ + int storage   │          │          ├──────────┤
│ + bool running  │   0..1    │ + String ID       │
│ + List services │           │ + Hash resources  │
└─────────────────┘           │ [+ int costs]     │
                              └───────────────────┘
"ID":{
    "cluster": "1",
    "type": "ProcUnit",
    "vapp": "WebApp",
    "cpu": 34,
    "mem": 25,
    "hdd": 70,
    "running": True,
    "services": ["nginx", "app"]  }
```

Plans denote the solutions computed by the automated planning algorithm. A final solution plan consists of primitive tasks that are no longer decomposable. Each plan has a set of effects which are expected post–conditions after the execution of the solution.

```
           1..*                      1..*
┌──────────┐        ┌──────────────────┐
│ Plan     │        │ Effect           │
├──────────┤        ├──────────────────┤
│ + String ID│      │ + String ID      │
│ + List Tasks│     │ + Status Est_Status│
└──────────┘        └──────────────────┘
"PlanID": {
  "actions":[
  {TASK_1},
  {TASK_2},
  ... ],
  "effect":[
  {NEW_STATUS} ] },
```

Management Tasks encode knowledge on recovery actions. Two types of tasks are presented in this model: Abstract Task denotes high level tasks that could be further refined into more specific actions; Task describes primitive action that is atomic and directly implementable.

```
┌────────────────────┐        ┌──────────────────┐
│ Abstract Task      │   *    │ Task             │
├────────────────────┤  1..*  ├──────────────────┤
│ + String name      │        │ + String ID      │
│ + precondition :   │        │ + precondition : │
│   List[Hash]       │        │   List[Hash]     │
│ + List operations  │        │ + String action  │
│ + String vmtype    │        └──────────────────┘
└────────────────────┘
"TASK_ID": {
  "preconditions": \
  [{"overload": true}],
  "todo": \
  ["clone", "migrate"],
  "type": 0,
  "name": "CreateNewDB",
  "vmtype": ["database"]
},
```

A planning problem is denoted as a $P = (\Sigma, s_0, g)$, where $\Sigma = (S, A, \gamma)$ is a representation of a state-transition system with states $s_i \in S$, a set of selectable (management) actions $a_i \in A$ with pre- and post-conditions $a_i^{pre} \subseteq S$ and $a_i^{post} \subseteq S$, a state-transition function γ, a current state s_0 and a goal state g. When multiple recovery paths are available for the planner to choose from, a cost function $c(a_i, s_i) > 0$ is needed for comparison of costs of the action a_i associated with the state s_i.

A solution to a planning problem P is a sequence of actions $(a_1, \ldots, a_k), k \leq n$, which effects the transition between s_0 to the goal state. The state-transition function γ maps (i.e. binds) actions to transitions, $s_1 = \gamma(s_0, a_1), \ldots, s_n = \gamma(s_{n-1}, a_n)$.

A naïve planning algorithm could in principle find a plan by searching the complete space of possible states; but the typical execution time of such an algorithm would exceed any time-frame practical in IT management. We argue that the HTN-based (hierarchical task network) planning paradigm is the best choice for fault recovery planning problem. HTN planners recursively decompose high-level tasks into subtasks until primitive tasks result, which are equivalent to atomic management actions. We briefly compare planning strategies in Section 5.

Four groups of information items comprise the knowledge required to support automated planning. Table 1 describes these groups more in-depth and shows the concrete models employed in our prototype evaluation along with example value sets.

3.4 Planning Algorithm

Algorithm 1 uses instances of the discussed knowledge items and produces a plan, i.e. a sequence of atomic actions. It is common practices in AI planning to apply heuristics in order to accelerate the planning process. Empirical experience [13] shows that for most applications of automated planning of real-world problems, near-optimal solutions can do quite well.

In order to reduce the time-to-solution, our algorithm combines the HTN planning approach with a *best-first* search procedure similar to the hill-climbing heuristic [10].

The planning algorithm is parameterised with `status` and `tasklist` variables. The description of the current state model of a service (e.g. the *WebApp*) is represented by a `status` parameter, which includes current CPU and memory utilisation as well as available storage of involved virtual resources. Additionally, the types of services and special conditions can be also included in the status description. The tasks of the solution are stored in the `tasklist` data structure during recursion through different task levels.

The algorithm begins with an empty *statuslist* intended to hold all potential states that can be generated from the current state. The potential states are those reachable by applying recovery tasks.

Algorithm 1. First best search planner with heuristic estimate evaluation.

```
 1: function dig(status, tasklist)              19:          else
 2:     statuslist ← ∅                          20:              statuslist  ←  statuslist +
 3:     currenteval ← EVALUATE(status)              (newstatus, appended)
 4:     for vm in status do                    21:          end if
 5:         tasks ← GETTASKS(vm)                22:      end for
 6:         for task in tasks do               23:  end for
 7:             if task is decomposable then   24:  filter  statuslist  for  evaluation  ≤
 8:                 refine task                     currenteval
 9:                 for t in refined task do   25:  if statuslist is ∅ then
10:                     newstatus ← APPLY(t, vm)  26:      SolutionNotFoundError
11:                 end for                    27:  end if
12:             else                           28:  sort  statuslist  ascending  on  value  of
13:                 newstatus ← apply(task, vm)     evaluation
14:             end if                         29:  return dig(state, tasklist[0])
15:             neweval ← EVALUATE(newstatus)  30:  if SolutionNotFoundError then
16:             appended ← tasklist + task     31:      process next possible solution
17:             if neweval = 0 then            32:  end if
18:                 return appended            33: end function
```

The EVALUATE function analyses the current global state (provided by the status parameter) and classifies the states of individual virtual resources into one of the fault states: *hangup, idle, stopped* or *missing*. These potential states (simply represented by integer values in our implementation) are determined by symptoms apparent in monitoring data collected from the virtual infrastructure. More sophisticated evaluation heuristics or utility functions could be applied, see e.g. [8], to get more precise classification results.

The algorithm iteratively searches for viable recovery tasks for the involved virtual resource taking into account the pre-conditions provided as part of recovery knowledge. If a selected task is decomposable, it is then further refined according to the "hints" (in the form of a task network) present in the task description.

The APPLY function commits the selected atomic actions to the current state model and transits the model into a new state. Effects of atomic (executable) tasks that would change the current state of the observed virtual resource are reflected as state changes in the statuslist. This new state is passed to the EVALUATE function to achieve a new set of possible configurations. The configurations with the best estimation value are then further extended by the recursive call of the planning function (dig). The recursion ends when the estimated value is below the pre-defined threshold (i.e. there are no further candidates).

Note that at each level of expansion, only the recovery configuration with best evaluation is further processed by the algorithm. The rest of the possible configuration will be pruned for the purpose of efficiency.

4   Prototypical Implementation and Evaluations

The algorithm is prototyped in Python and the knowledge on system states, descriptions of recovery tasks and system are represented in JSON[1] (JavaScript Object Notation, RFC 4627), a light-weight, language-independent information interchange format.

The evaluation is based on simulations performed on data collected from an operational virtualized environment. The tests were performed on a Linux machine with a 2.2 GHz CPU and 3 GB memory. For each test in different test groups, around 10 tests are conducted. Figure 3 shows the evaluation results with standard deviations for each data point.

We test the scalability of our approach with respect to three dimensions: number of VMs, types of faults and length of plan.

In the first experiment, we scale from 15 to 300 VMs and inject 6 different types of faults into the test data. In the first test configuration in Figure 3(a) the algorithm has a steep growth on the landmark of approximately 150 VMs in a service. This behaviour is caused by the fact that the algorithm initially expands an increasing number of search nodes as the number of machines grows. A possible remedy to this problem is using dynamic programming or caching techniques. We consider the runtime of approximately 4 minutes to find a fault recovery solution in a service involving about 300 VMs to be an acceptable time frame in real operations.

---

[1] http://tools.ietf.org/html/rfc4627

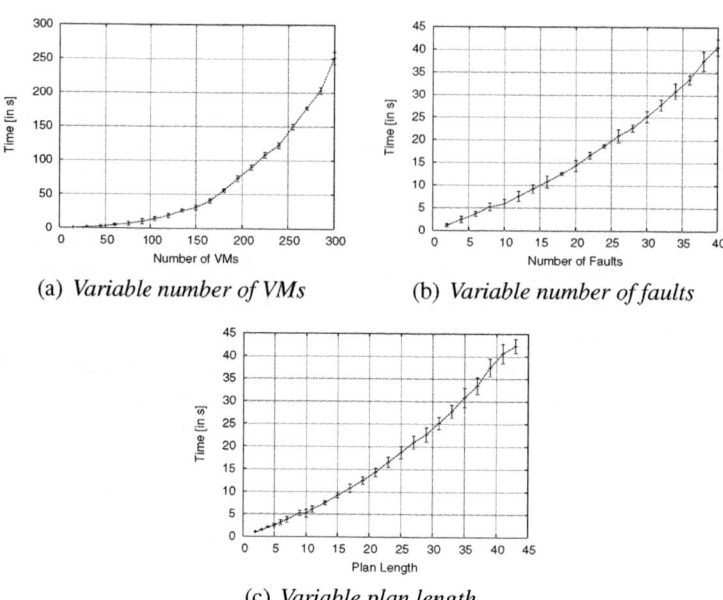

(a) *Variable number of VMs*   (b) *Variable number of faults*

(c) *Variable plan length*

Fig. 3. Evaluation results of various test configurations

```
"task": {                    "task": {                    "task": {
  "todo": "restart",           "todo": "restart",           "todo": "delete",
  "preconditions":             "preconditions":             "preconditions": [],
    [{"running": 1}],            [{"running": 1}],           "type": 1
  "type": 1},                  "type": 1                   },
"params": {                  },                           "params": {
  "amount": 1,               "params": {                    "amount": 1,
  "app": "WebApp",             "amount": 2,                 "app": "WebApp",
  "type": "ProcUnit",          "app": "WebApp",             "type": "ProcUnit",
  "id": "VM_204"               "type": "ProcUnit",          "id": "VM_369"
},                             "id": "VM_680"              },
"vm": "VM_204",              },                           "vm": "VM_369",
"level": 0                   "vm": "VM_680",              "level": 4
                             "level": 2

"task": {                    "task": {                    "task": {
  "todo": "restart",           "todo": "deploy",            "todo": "delete",
  "preconditions":             "preconditions": [],         "preconditions": [],
    [{"running": 1}],          "type": 1                   "type": 1
  "type": 1},                },                           },
"params": {                  "params": {                  "params": {
  "amount": 1,                 "amount": 2,                 "amount": 1,
  "app": "WebApp",             "app": "WebApp",             "app": "WebApp",
  "type": "ProcUnit",          "type": "ProcUnit",          "type": "ProcUnit",
  "id": "VM_69"                "id": "VM_595"               "id": "VM_237"
},                           },                           },
"vm": "VM_69",               "vm": "VM_595",              "vm": "VM_237",
"level": 1                   "level": 3                   "level": 5
```

Fig. 4. Example of a plan output

In a second test, we variate the number of faults injected into the test data ranging from 2 to 40 faults while using a constant number of 50 virtual machines. Implicitly we change the length of resulting plans to up to 40 steps. The results shown in Figures 3(b),3(c) suggest that runtime growth is quicker in the presence of larger number of faults.

Small deviations in all collected data points suggest a relatively stable and predictable behaviour of the algorithm. The bottleneck of the algorithm lays in the initial expansion of the search tree. The further deep searches of the selected nodes with best evaluation results are accelerated by the recovery knowledge encoded in the task description.

Figure 4 shows an example output of one of the test cases, which involves *WebApp* running on a PaaS platform. The injected faults simulate cases in which three virtual Processing Units (PU) do not process the user requests but still are in running state and showing exceptionally high CPU and memory usages. Another two PUs have unknown and unretrievable states. These faults are injected in the state description data. The algorithm rates the first three PUs as corrupted and decides to select `restart` as recovery actions. For the latter two PUs, the algorithm decides to deploy two instance PUs of same type to replace the missing ones and deletes the unresponsive instances.

5   Related Work

Our survey of related work indicates that the research of the applications of AI planning techniques in IT management is just emerging, in particular in the domain of fault management of virtualized infrastructures like cloud computing installations.

Planning techniques in IT management. Arshad et al. [3] propose a plan based fault recovery in distributed systems based on a state based planner which limits the effectively computable problem sizes. Gopisetty et al. [15] suggest a provisioning and recovery system limited storage systems. The recovery mechanism uses knowledge base for the planning purposes, but an encoding scheme is missing. Robertson et al. [14] present early work on a model based error recovery for robotic systems, however their approach is focused on the embedded software systems for robots, the modeling of planning environment is therefore focused on the geographic terrain informations for robot movement.

Although not directly related to fault management, some interesting research is found in Grid research. Andrzejak et al. [2] recognise the importance of planning support for self-adapting Grid infrastructures. They envision an algorithm supported planning system that empowers the Grid computing infrastructure to be self-managing. Blythe et al. [4,5] applied planning for automated configuration of Grid-based applications which concentrates on finding composition plans for the optimal solutions. They sacrifice the planning time for the quality of the plan which may be acceptable in configuration management, but not in fault recovery.

Planning Paradigms. A common critique of applying automated planning techniques to solve real-world problem falls upon its computational complexity as the problem size grows. We select a HTN-based approach, as the classical planners such as state-based or plan-based planners [12] are often described as merely suitable to solve "toy problems" with restricted sizes.

HTN-based planning algorithms are efficient: both theoretical studies [7] and empirical experience [9] show that such planners can achieve significant performance gains over other planners. Additionally, the HTN-based planners proved to be sound and complete in algorithmic perspective of view [12,6], i.e. they will find a correct solution if one exists.

Our choice in favour of HTN planning for the benefit of IT fault management was motivated by two factors: First, the hierarchical plan structure resembles how humans solve complex practical problems by decomposing high-level tasks; this allows a natural mapping of management actions to planner tasks. Second, the characteristic constructs such as *abstract tasks* allow integration of recovery knowledge into the planning process allow knowledge reuse. In turn, this allows reduction of the time cost of the planning operation for the benefit of the quality of the solution.

6   Conclusions and Future Work

In this paper we proposed a architecture and process for automated fault recovery, based on a planning algorithm and machine-readable knowledge about the state of the managed system. We evaluated the prototypical implementation of the algorithm by means of simulations driven by data collected in a live operational environment. The evaluation of different test configurations shows encouraging results and suggest that automated planning is, indeed, a viable technique for use in IT management. The prototype discussed appears to scale well to a higher number of (potentially faulty) resources but is sensitive to the number of actual concurrent faults. We note that effective plan-based management depends not only on a planning algorithm but also on the availability and quality of management knowledge; effective monitoring and actuation components are a prerequisite.

Real-life deployment of such an approach entails taking into account temporal and financial constraints on fault recovery, such as prioritisation by service, customer or criticality, elapsed down-time, financial service penalties and so on. The planning and execution time for the recovery of a fault may be short, but new, additional faults may occur during that time, thus rendering the state of the infrastructure uncertain; re-planning strategies are necessary to address such occurrences. Also, the required information (i.e. knowledge) about the infrastructure may be incomplete, thus demanding an approach to generate and manage partial plans. Finally, HTN planning can be optimised by a variety of heuristics and evaluation functions; an investigation of alternatives may yield a more efficient planner for the domain of fault recovery.

Acknowledgment

The authors wish to thank the members of the Munich Network Management Team (MNM Team) for helpful discussions and valuable comments on previous versions of this paper. The MNM Team directed by Prof. Dr. Dieter Kranzlmüller and Prof. Dr. Heinz-Gerd Hegering is a group of researchers at Ludwig-Maximilians-Universität München, Technische Universität München, the University of the Federal Armed Forces and the Leibniz Supercomputing Centre of the Bavarian Academy of Science. http://www.mnm-team.org

References

1. Willams, A.: Top 5 Cloud Outages of the Past Two Years. ReadWrite Cloud (2010)
2. Andrzejak, A., Reinefeld, A., Schintke, F., Schuett, T.: On adaptability in grid systems. Future Generation Grids, 29–46 (2006)
3. Arshad, N.: A Planning-Based Approach to Failure Recovery in Distributed Systems. PhD thesis, University of Colorado at Boulder (2006)
4. Blythe, J., Deelman, E., Gil, Y., Kesselman, C.: Transparent grid computing: a knowledge-based approach. In: 15th Innovative Applications of Artificial Intelligence Conference (2003)
5. Deelman, E., Blythe, J., Gil, Y., Kesselman, K.V.C., Mehta, G.: Mapping abstract complex workflows onto grid environments. Journal of Grid Computing 1(1) (March 2003)
6. Erol, K., Hendler, J., Nau, D.S.: Umcp: A sound and complete procedure for hierarchical task-network planning. In: Proceedings of the 2nd International Conference on Artificial Intelligence Planning Systems (AIPS 1994), pp. 249–254 (1994)
7. Barrett, A., et al.: Partial-order planning: Evaluating possible efficiency gains. Artificial Intelligence 67, 71–112 (1994)
8. Fishburn, P.C.: Utility theory for decision making. Storming Media (1970)
9. Fox, M., Long, D.: International planning competition (2002)
10. Goldberg, D.E., et al.: Genetic algorithms in search, optimization, and machine learning. Addison-Wesley, Reading (1989)
11. Dignan, L.: Amazon's S3 Outage: Is the cloud too complicated? ZDNet (July 2008)
12. Nau, D., Ghallab, M., Traverso, P.: Automated Planning: Theory & Practice. Morgan Kaufmann Publishers Inc., San Francisco (2004)
13. Nau, D.S.: Current trends in automated planning. AI Magazine 28(4), 43 (2007)
14. Robertson, P., Williams, B.: Automatic recovery from software failure. Communications of the ACM 49(3), 47 (2006)
15. Gopisetty, S., et al.: Automated Planner for Storage Provisioning and Disaster Recovery. IBM Journal of Research and Development 52(4/5) (2008)

Author Index

GPSR Compliance

The European Union's (EU) General Product Safety Regulation (GPSR) is a set of rules that requires consumer products to be safe and our obligations to ensure this.

If you have any concerns about our products, you can contact us on ProductSafety@springernature.com

In case Publisher is established outside the EU, the EU authorized representative is:

Springer Nature Customer Service Center GmbH
Europaplatz 3
69115 Heidelberg, Germany

Batch number: 09478804

Printed by Printforce, the Netherlands